# Completing Distinctions

# Completing Distinctions

DOUGLAS G. FLEMONS

Foreword by Bradford P. Keeney, Ph.D.

SHAMBHALA
Boston & London
1991

SHAMBHALA PUBLICATIONS, INC.
Horticultural Hall
300 Massachusetts Avenue
Boston, Massachusetts 02115
*www.shambhala.com*

Printed in the United States of America

Distributed in the United States by Random House, Inc.,
and in Canada by Random House of Canada Ltd

LIBRARY OF CONGRESS CATALOGING-IN-PUBLICATION DATA

Flemons, Douglas G.
    Completing distinctions / Douglas G. Flemons.—1st ed.
      p.  cm.
    Includes bibliographical references
    ISBN: 1-57062-669-3
      1. Family psychotherapy.   2. Taoism.   3. Bateson, Gregory.  I. Title.
  RC488.5.F58   1990                           89-43611
  616.89'156—dc20                          CIP

Design by Melodie Wertelet

BVG 01

TO MY TEACHERS

Between what I see and what I say,
between what I say and what I keep silent,
between what I keep silent and what I dream,
between what I dream and what I forget:
poetry.
     It slips
between yes and no,
            says
what I keep silent,
            keeps silent
what I say,
       dreams
what I forget.
        It is not speech:
it is an act.
       It is an act
of speech.
      Poetry
speaks and listens:
           it is real.
And as soon as I say
         *it is real,*
it vanishes.
      Is it then more real?

—*Octavio Paz*
*(translated by Eliot Weinberger)*

# CONTENTS

# FOREWORD

Gregory Bateson once proposed that "it takes two to know one." His preference for doubleness provided us with a desire to emphasize *relationship* over things. What was too easily forgotten, however, was that double views, double hearings, double acts, and double takes only lead to the relational realization of "things." A distinction between two may be closed (or completed) to become one.

To know two, extending this logic of relationship, necessarily requires the presence of *three*. Whereas Bateson's double lens paradoxically takes us to "things," a triple somersault is necessary to see relationship. This next big jump moves us from tossing two balls to juggling at least three.

It is precisely at this point that the master juggler Douglas Flemons enters the scene. In his remarkable book, he advances the Batesonian tradition beyond the game of two. In one hand he releases the ancient tradition of Taoism. In the other hand we find the more contemporary insights of Batesonian cybernetic epistemology. Caught in midair between the other two is the ever-present question and discipline of how to therapeutically address human problems. In his juggle, we derive deeper understandings of each perspective through the dancing flight of all three.

Our juggling author, upon closer examination, can be seen in this text as actually juggling three parts of himself. Douglas Flemons is, in fact, a practicing Taoist, a systemic therapist, and a cybernetic epistemologist (not to mention that he is also an accomplished juggler!). What is recorded in this text is most fascinating: the juggler being juggled.

Three traditions of ideas and practices toss our author into a recursive flight of abstractions weaving in and out of one another. What is cooked, to borrow a metaphor from Stewart Brand, is a most satisfying slice of mental baklava.

Reader, think twice (make that thrice) about entering the spins of the following pages. It is not for the passive onlooker. This text invites the reader to participate in its movement. The rhetorical juggling of Douglas Flemons doesn't require that *you* catch anything. It sets up the possibility of your being caught in its dance of intertwined separations and connections, including the difference and relation between the reader, the read, and the ever-moving voice of the author. Three cheers for a magnificent performance.

BRADFORD P. KEENEY, PH.D.
College of St. Thomas
St. Paul, Minnesota

# ACKNOWLEDGMENTS

It was my brother Tom, inveterate scout that he is, who first acquainted me with Eastern philosophy and introduced me to the sinologist and teacher Titus Yü. Titus patiently guided me into and through the eliptical world of Taoism and offered me the opportunity to collaborate with him on an etymologically grounded translation of an ancient Chinest text; the learnings gleaned from our years of working together in the late 1970s and early '80s are woven throughout the present book.

Anthony Wilden piqued my interest in, and contributed to my understanding of, the work of Gregory Bateson. I found Bateson's notions helpful as I puzzled over Taoist writings, and Taoist thought helpful as I mused over Bateson's essays. This circling juxtaposition of ideas has stayed with me as a method of inquiry, and I have incorporated it in this book as a method of explanation.

Through his teaching of the martial art T'ai Chi Ch'üan, Master Raymond Chung helped me, over the years, to appreciate and incorporate Taoist principles in ways that would have otherwise been impossible.

Anyone familiar with the scholarship of Brad Keeney will recognize my tremendous debt to his work, particularly to his *Aesthetics of Change* (1983), where many of the important voices that I drew on in the writing of this book—including Gregory Bateson, Francisco Varela, Wendell Berry, Gary Snyder, and Heinz von Foerster—were first brought together. As Brad's student, and later as his colleague, I deepened my understanding of Bateson and learned much about the practice of therapy and the discipline of improvisation.

The discerning comments and suggestions of my editor at Shambhala Publications, Jeremy Hayward, contributed greatly to the clarity of the final draft. Jeremy and the others at Shambhala—especially Peter Turner and Jonathan Green—created a most supportive ambiance for the completion of the manuscript.

Moyra Jones was an important source of inspiration and a perceptive critic. Larry Cochran was perhaps the first to suggest that my interests in Bateson, Taoism, and therapy could be successfully entwined. David and Kathee Todtman broke trail for my trek to Texas, where much of the idea development and part of the writing took place. They offered intellectual stimulation and warm friendship, along with great cappuccino.

My friends and colleagues at Nova University—Ron Chenail, Sharon Boesl, Anne and Bill Rambo, John Flynn, Wendel Ray, Loren Bryant, and Marguerite McCorkle—each contributed to the text in unique and important ways. Their comments, digging up of sources, reading of drafts, and many other kindnesses are deeply appreciated. Ron, with his thoughtful mind and expansive library, was particularly helpful. Connie Steele, at the University of Tennessee at Knoxville, closely read an earlier draft and made a number of pertinent suggestions.

The questions asked by my students have encouraged me to think and speak more clearly. The questions posed by my clients have challenged me to work and play more imaginatively.

Shelley Green, Jerry and Barbara Gale, and the Braudt family provided long-distant, but closely felt support.

My parents and my brothers stood behind me all the way. To them, and to everyone else, I offer my heartfelt thanks.

# Completing Distinctions

# 1 | The Relation Between

l(a

le
af
fa

ll

s)

one
l

iness

—*e. e. cummings*

DAUGHTER  I did an experiment once.
FATHER  Yes?
DAUGHTER  I wanted to find out if I could think two thoughts at the same time. So I thought "It's summer" and I thought "It's winter." And then I tried to think the two thoughts together.
FATHER  Yes?
DAUGHTER  But I found I wasn't having two thoughts. I was only having one thought *about* having two thoughts.

—*Gregory Bateson*

Any act of knowing, any knowing act, begins with the drawing of a distinction, with the noting of a difference. A boundary is created when a whole is distinguished from a part of itself—as in ecosystem/species, paragraph/sentence, family/child—or when a part of a whole is simply differentiated from another part—as in foreground/background, yesterday/tomorrow, husband/wife. The relationship formed by such acts of demarcation constitute the "stuff" of mind. Knowing is composed of boundaries imposed.

It is to the exploration of this fascinating, relational nature of mind—and its implications for the art of living and the practice of therapy—that much of this book is devoted.

The Taoists and Buddhists were perhaps the first to recognize that in the marking of a difference, the boundary that *separates* the two sides of the created distinction necessarily *connects* them. However, this relational insight also runs as an undercurrent through the work of Gregory Bateson, as well as of Francisco Varela, George Spencer-Brown, Wendell Berry, Gary Snyder, and others. A most interesting conceptual tool spirals into form if this instance of distinctive understanding is allowed to pivot on itself. The distinction *connection/separation* describes the doubleness of the relation between the two sides of a difference, and in so doing it comments on itself, as it connects and separates connection and separation.

It is thus that the introductory poem and conversation—and their juxtaposition—prefigure much of what is to follow. A leaf falls, parenthetical to the invocation of loneliness: "l (a/ le/af/fa/ ll/ s)/one/l/ iness." The syncopated symmetry of the leaf's descent is not described but inscribed by the shape and the time of the telling. Each line depicts part of the story, as the leaf dips first this way—"le"—then that—"af"—and then reverses back—"fa"—before pausing, fluttering—"ll"—pausing again, and continuing down.

Loneliness speaks of isolation, of separation. It begins and then completes the rhythm of the leaf's fall—"l . . . /one/ l/ iness"—and in so doing establishes a resonance: The insularity of loneliness and the singularity of the detached leaf are each metaphoric of the other. It is the connection between these two expressions of separateness that sparks meaning in the poem, that brings it poignantly to life.

William Carlos Williams says mind and poem "are all apiece." As the daughter in the quote from Bateson came to realize, mind, like a poem, always weaves. The act of thinking two disparate thoughts—such as "it's winter" and "it's summer"—necessarily ties the two of them together. The attempt to separate is itself a connection. The form in which this idea is presented mirrors what is said: There is one conversation between two "distinct" people about "having one thought about having two 'distinct' thoughts." The interchange between father and daughter is excerpted from one of Bateson's *metalogues*, a type of dialogue where "not only do the participants discuss [a] problem but the structure of the conversation as a whole is also relevant to the same subject." [1]

Form and content rhyme; connection and separation entwine. Such is the unique pattern of each of the quoted passages and of the connections between them. At still a more encompassing level, it is descriptive of the structure of this book as a whole. Like a poem or a metalogue, it will attend to the coincidence of meaning and the manner of its expression: The distinction *connection/separation* will be used as a relational map with which to explore the relationally mapped ideas of Bateson and of Taoist philosophers, and to chart a relational orientation to therapy. The path taken will not be direct, but will cycle, spinning and looping, turning and returning its way within and between these three domains of knowing and acting.

The company is not as strange as might first appear. In a sense Bateson plays host to the other two, despite the fact that he never wrote about Oriental philosophy and had serious reservations about the whole enterprise of therapy. Common to all three is an awareness of, and a sensitivity to, levels of context and meaning, and an understanding of how these levels interconnect in intricate and often paradoxical ways.

Although Bateson never wrote *about* Taoism and Zen Buddhism per se, ideas from both traditions are interspersed throughout his writings,[2] and, indeed, his systemic approach to mind has a distinct Oriental flavor. Bateson first started talking about Zen practice in the 1950s,[3] at a time when he was "picking the brains" of Alan Watts,[4] and although he remained peripheral to it, he maintained ties to the San Francisco Zen community up until his death in 1980: He spent his last few days and died, at the age of seventy-six, in the guest house of the San Francisco Zen Center.[5] Bateson respected the vision of the artist and the mystic; but he considered himself a scientist, and worked and wrote in that tradition. It is thus not surprising that he would begin a talk at The Naropa Institute in 1975 in the following way: "What I want to say, quite simply, is that what goes on inside is much the same as what goes on outside. And I say this not from anything like a Buddhist position, but just from the position of an ordinary working stiff engaged in Occidental sciences."[6]

Bateson was hardly "an ordinary working stiff," and his scientific focus was far from traditional. Devoting his rapt attention to "the pattern which connects," his varied excursions into the fields of anthropology, biology, communication theory, psychiatry, evolutionary theory, ecology, and aesthetics were in the service of the development of a new "epistemology," that is, "an indivisible, integrated meta-science whose subject matter is the world of evolution, thought, adaptation, embryology, and genetics—the science of mind in the widest sense of the word."[7] The metaphor of "mind" provided for him a means of characterizing the circuitous relations that obtain between the parts of a system and between systems.

The beginnings of this and many related ideas can be traced to his involvement in the cross-disciplinary Macy conferences, held in New York during the late 1940s and early 1950s. These meetings provided a unique forum where innovations from mathematics and engineering were rigorously applied to a variety of other fields.[8] Focusing on the nature of "circular causal and feedback mechanisms in biological and social systems," the talks marked the formal beginning of the science of cybernetics, the study of the organization of systems in terms of communicational pathways and self-corrective patterns of circular process.[9]

Considering cybernetics to be "the biggest bite out of the fruit of the Tree of Knowledge that mankind has taken in the last 2000 years,"[10] Bateson adopted and adapted many of its key notions, including Bertrand Russell's Theory of Logical Types, circular causality, entropy, negative and positive feedback, the distinction between analogical and digital processes, and between information and energy.[11] As important contributions to the development of his "science of mind," these cybernetic ideas warrant explanation; the definitions that follow can perhaps serve as cairns to help mark the direction of Bateson's trail.

1. Russell's *Theory of Logical Types* distinguishes between levels of abstraction. Originally invented as a way of eschewing paradox in the world of logic, the notion of logical types is used by Bateson as a way of charting the classification inherent in all perceiving, thinking, learning, and communicating. A class is a different logical type, a higher level of abstraction, than the members it classifies: The class of "all books" is itself not a book; the name of a thing is itself not a thing, but a classification of it. At a still more abstract level, the class of "classes of rectangular objects," which would include the class of books, the class of cereal boxes, the class of picture frames, and so on, is not itself a class of rectangular objects, but a way of classifying these classes, and as such is a higher logical type. The name of the name is not the name. This hierarchy of types—classes, classes of classes, classes of classes of classes, and so on—provides a convenient bridge to the critical notion of *context* and the interdependence of wholes and parts. The notion of levels makes clear that learning, for example, is a contextual affair; one not only learns, but simultaneously learns how to

learn. Similarly, according to Bateson, "the very process of perception is an act of logical typing. Every image is a complex of many-leveled coding and mapping." [12]

2. *Lineal causality,* where "A causes B," is but a partial arc of the circuitous relations that obtain in the world of ongoing interaction. *Circular causality* refers to the reciprocal nature of systemic process: A responds to B's response to A, to which B, in turn, responds, and so on.

3. In contradistinction to *pattern,* which is connected to notions of order, redundancy, and organization, *entropy* refers to disorder, randomness, and muddle.

4. The term *feedback* is descriptive of the loop structure of systems, whereby information from or about the system returns to it, thereby influencing the shape of the circuit. Whereas *positive feedback* changes the system's stability (as in the spiral of schismogenic runaway), *negative feedback* stabilizes the system's changing (as in the circle of self-corrective homeostasis).

5. Each step in a communicational sequence is a transform of the previous step. In *digital* communication, such as written (and verbal) language, there is no formal connection between a sign and that of which it is a transform: The word *mountain* is no taller than the word *valley;* the word *sun* is no brighter or hotter than the word *shade;* and there is nothing particularly lionlike about the word *lion.* In *analogical* communication, such as kinesics and paralinguistics, magnitudes are used to code magnitudes, and there is thus a recognizable connection between the transform and that which it re-presents: A lowered voice, long pause, raised eyebrow, or expansive gesture will generally correspond (directly or inversely) to a magnitude in the relationship to which it refers.

6. *Energy* belongs to the world of substance, to quantities and things, impacts and forces; *information* belongs to the world of form, to relationship, pattern, and organization. Distinguishing between information and energy is itself an

informational act, in that it defines a *difference:* Information is, in Bateson's terms, a difference which makes a difference.

A cairn, like a pointed finger, takes on significance not when it captures one's attention, but when it directs it elsewhere. Similarly, an idea becomes most important not when it answers a previous question, but when it makes possible the asking of the next one. These cybernetic ideas allowed Bateson to ask fascinating questions about the nature of mind. From 1952 to 1962, he directed a series of research projects which investigated levels of abstraction and paradox in communication. He and collaborators John Weakland and Jay Haley, with William Fry and Don Jackson as consultants, studied everything from ventriloquism and the training of guide dogs for the blind, to humor, play, hypnosis, and schizophrenic communication. Of the many important theoretical ideas developed during the course of the project, the notion of the double bind was preeminent, and once it had been formulated, in 1954, it served to direct subsequent inquiry.

The double bind provides a contextual way of describing the complexity of conflicting demands across different levels of context. If solving a problem of learning or adaptation at one contextual level thereby creates a problem at a more encompassing contextual level (thus undermining the original solution), the tangled situation as a whole can be described as a double bind: "The organism is then faced with the dilemma either of being wrong in the primary context or of being right for the wrong reasons or in a wrong way."[13]

The matter can also be approached in terms of the way in which freedom is determined. As any good hypnotist, magician, or comedian knows, the offer or availability of freely choosing between alternatives at a given contextual level brings the particularities of choice into the foreground of conscious awareness. This necessarily relegates to the background (i.e., out of awareness and out of the realm of conscious choice) the higher-level *context* or *premise* determining the range and meaning of the offered alternatives. The presence of choice (between particularities) at one level masks—and in some sense precludes—choice (between premises) at a more encompassing level. The theory of the double bind found particular illustration in the paradoxical patterns and learning contexts of schizophrenic communication,[14] but Bateson considered its formal characteristics capable of handling the contextual complexity of a host of other relational phenomena, including play, learning, psychotherapy, humor, art, religion, hypnosis, dreams, creativity, addiction, adaptation, and the processes of evolution.[15]

Description embeds prescription—or as Bateson would say, all communication has a dual aspect: "Every message in transit has two sorts of 'meaning.' On the one hand, the message is a statement or report about events at a previous moment, and on the other hand it is a command—a cause or stimulus for events at a later moment."[16] Although the double bind was not advanced as a theory of therapy—it says nothing, for example, of how a therapist should conduct a session—the contextual view it proposed carried certain therapeutic implications. Over the ten-year course of the Bateson project, the researchers, as part of their interest in the communicational nature of psychiatry, regularly saw patients for therapy; however, there was a shift about midway through the project from working with individuals to treating whole families.[17] This significant move helped launch the field of family therapy. According to Bateson:

> Family therapy . . . denotes more than the introduction of a new method and more than a mere shift in the size of the social unit with which the therapist feels he must deal. Indeed, the very change in the size of the unit brings with it a new epis-

temology and ontology, i.e., a new way of thinking about what a *mind* is and a new concept of man's place in the world.[18]

Although Bateson saw patients from 1948 to 1963,[19] he did not consider himself a clinician. First and foremost a theorist, he was interested in such subjects as alcoholism, schizophrenia, and psychotherapy not as phenomena in and of themselves, but as "examples of formal relations, which will illustrate a theory."[20] As he put it: "I do not need schizophrenic patients or unhappy families to give my thinking empirical roots. I can use art, poetry or porpoises or the cultures of New Guinea and Manhattan, or my own dreams or the comparative anatomy of flowering plants."[21]

Bateson saw therapy as a species of applied science, and he was deeply wary of its instrumentality: "We social scientists would do well to hold back our eagerness to control that world which we so imperfectly understand."[22] Indeed, he was far from pleased with the ways his ideas were generally translated (he would probably have said "corrupted") into therapeutic theory and practice.[23] The spirit of, and reasons for, his rancor are nicely caught in a metalogue written by Mary Catherine Bateson; in it, her father is withering in his condemnation of the field.

> FATHER  There's still . . . the problem of the misuse of ideas. The engineers get hold of them. Look at the whole god-awful business of family therapy, therapists making "paradoxical interventions" in order to change people or families, or counting "double binds." You can't count double binds.[24]

Attempting to enumerate double binds is rather like trying to count the humor in a comedian's monologue—there is no localizable "thing" to itemize. As with humor, double binds characterize the multilevel relationship within and between statements and between participants in an exchange.

The "paradoxing" of clients to which (Gregory) Bateson refers speaks of manipulation, a purposeful act which tears the contextual fabric of relationship:

> A screwdriver is not seriously affected when, in an emergency, we use it as a wedge; and a hammer's outlook on life is not affected because we sometimes use its handle as a simple lever. But in social manipulation our tools are people, and people learn, and they acquire habits which are more subtle and pervasive than the tricks which the blueprinter teaches them.[25]

A little later in her metalogue, Mary Catherine Bateson suggests how family therapy, a field that, after all, developed out of an appreciation of the importance of contextual integrity, might have gone awry:

> DAUGHTER   See, what I think is going on is the same process that produces the monstrous beetles with extra limbs,[26] the same thing is creating a monstrousness in the family-therapy industry, and other places too. Some of the information has been lost, an essential part of the idea.[27]

This suggestion introduces a number of pressing questions. What critical information is missing? And can the rent be repaired? It would be naive to assume that a particular lacuna could simply be localized, analyzed, and then appropriately sewn up. As in genetic coding, "a single *bit* of information—a single difference—may be the yes-or-no answer to a question of any degree of complexity, at any level of abstraction."[28] At what contextual level, then, has family therapy gone off track? Are some clinicians, some schools less "monstrous," less inclined to quantify patterns and chop up ecologies? Is all theory implicated, all practice tainted? Are there bits and pieces that are salvageable, or is the whole enterprise necessarily thrown into question? And even if we were able to identify particular problems, is there anything that can be done as a corrective?

The danger in addressing such questions and attempting to redress the problems they help identify is that one's actions may make the situation worse. One who attempts simply to "fix" a systemic situation, be it biological, societal, or familial, is poised from the outset to commit ecological blunders. When action is organized as a solution to a perceived or believed deficit, it necessarily becomes defined in opposition to that which is identified as a problem. The resulting mutual determination of problem and solution has the distinct potential of setting both in place. Gregory Bateson, in an interview with Stewart Brand, explains that any action stemming from the desire to do something—indeed, anything—as a corrective of "pathology" is fraught with difficulties. One is caught in a Taoist dilemma from the outset.

> The moment you want to ask the question, "What do you do about it?" that question itself chops the total ecology. I'm really talking Taoism, you know. The pathology is the breach of Taoism. And you say, "Well, now what's the cure for a breach of Taoism?" You want to say another breach of Taoism is the cure for it.[29]

A "breach of Taoism" is a rip in context. If the practice of change in family therapy is somehow destructive of the premises of relationship, so too can be attempts to change this practice of change:

> If you are carrying serious epistemological errors, you will find that they do not work any more. At this point you discover to your horror that it is exceedingly difficult to get rid of the error, that it's sticky. It is as if you had touched honey. As with honey, the falsification gets around; and each thing you try to wipe it off on gets sticky, and your hands still remain sticky.[30]

Having now been sounded, the questions about family therapy will be left to echo through the ensuing pages; however, they will not organize the form or content of what is to follow. Were they to be responded to directly, the premises contextualizing their articulation could not help but be embraced. The alternative is to inspire the imagination of a different class of question.

Taoist and Zen philosophers (as well as comedians, those labeled schizophrenic, and some therapists) are renowned for their deft ability to avoid being pinned down by the contextualizing nature of questions. Through metaphor, stories, absurdity, challenges, humor, and digression, they may offer an answer or pose another question, may indirectly comment on the category of question asked, and/or find ways to pose and answer questions of their own choosing. The Zen stories which follow are illuminating in this regard.

> One day a young novice said to Patriarch Hogen, "My name is Echo, and I would like to ask Your Reverence what is meant by the name Buddha?" Hogen merely said, "Oh so you are Echo are you?"

> A monk once asked Shozan, "Is there any phrase that is neither right nor wrong?" Shozan answered, "A piece of white cloud does not show any ugliness."

> Zuigan called out to himself every day, "Master." Then he answered himself, "Yes sir." And after that he added, "Become sober." Again he answered, "Yes sir." And after that he continued, "Do not be deceived by others." "Yes sir; yes sir," he answered.

> Nobushige, a soldier, came to Hakuin, a famous Zen Master, and asked, "Is there really a paradise and a hell?" "Who are you?" inquired Hakuin. "I am a samurai," Nobushige replied. "You, a samurai!" exclaimed Hakuin. "What kind of a lord would have you as his guard? You look like a beggar!" No-

bushige became so enraged that he began to draw his sword. Hakuin continued, "So you have a sword. It is probably too dull to even cut off my head." Nobushige brandished his weapon. Hakuin remarked, "Here, open the gates of hell." At these words the perceptive samurai sheathed his sword and bowed. "Here, open the gates of paradise," said Hakuin.[31]

There are many correspondences between Taoist and Zen (or, in Chinese, Ch'an) Buddhist thought. A number of writers attribute this to a historical confluence of the two traditions;[32] however, this presumption is open to question. Although reference will be made to some Zen writings in subsequent chapters, most of the focus will be on the Taoist works *Tao Te Ching, Chuang Tzu,* and *I Ching.*

The use of Chinese documents introduces the problem of translation. Never transparent, translation is at its best a transformation, a prism, defracting the original language and ideas in some kind of consistent way—and this, only if the text is interpreted within whatever is known of the cultural and historical context of its inception and with something of the original's linguistic integrity. It is beyond the scope of this work to provide a tour of the thought and language of ancient China; however, essential background will be provided when it contributes to a more thorough understanding of the ideas presented. A brief overview of the texts to be used may prove helpful.

It was the scholars of the Han dynasty (206 B.C.E.–220 C.E.) who first coined the term *Taoism* to encompass the philosophical doctrines of the *Tao Te Ching* and *Chuang Tzu.*[33] The authorship of the *Tao Te Ching* 道 德 經 ("book" 經 "of Tao" 道 "and te" 德) is traditionally attributed to Lao Tzu, said to have been an older contemporary of Confucius, living in the sixth century B.C.E. More recent scholarship suggests that the text should be considered an anthology dating to some time between the fifth and third cen-

turies B.C.E. The *Chuang Tzu* 莊子 bears the name of its re-
puted author, Chuang Tzu, who probably lived in the fourth
or third century B.C.E. His personal name is thought to have
been Chou, but little else is known about him, including the
part he played in writing "his" book—it too may be an anthology of sorts; at least some of the text was likely written
after his death.

The *I Ching* 易經 ("book" 經 "of change" 易) is
most certainly an assortment of layered texts, with the various parts compiled over the course of a millennium or more.
The earliest strata are generally thought to date to remote an-
tiquity, with later sections added at the beginning of the Chou
dynasty (circa 1100 B.C.E.) and Confucian appendices written perhaps as late as the beginning of the Han dynasty (circa
200 B.C.E.).[34] It could be argued that this book should not be
considered a Taoist text per se; nevertheless, it shares much of
the orientation of Taoism and may indeed have been the well-
spring for it.

Quotations from Lao Tzu's *Tao Te Ching* 道德經
("book" 經 "of Tao" 道 "and te" 德) will be mostly drawn
from John Wu's rendition; however, I will use other sources
and adapt certain phrases in ways which, in my view, better
accord with the laconic style of the original Chinese. If the
changes become more than just minor tinkering, I will explain
my rationale in an endnote. The passages from the *Chuang
Tzu* will come from Burton Watson's version, and those from *I
Ching* will be from Titus Yü's and my translation.[35]

The etymologies of Chinese characters can often be traced
back to pictograms, but there can be significantly different in-
terpretations of what the pictures originally represented. Unless otherwise indicated, my explanations of the meanings
and roots of Chinese characters will draw on the scholarship
of my teacher Titus Yü, who, in our work together, based his
analyses on many etymological dictionaries, most notably

Shuo Wen. Of course, I take responsibility for extrapolations and any omissions or errors.

Three of the characters in the titles of these Taoist texts give a hint of the richness of image found in the original language. The word *Tao* 道, found in the title and throughout the *Tao Te Ching*, depicts a foot 辶, which denotes movement, or, more specifically, "going and pausing,"[36] and a head 首, which symbolizes a person. Wieger says that the word as a whole means "to go ahead,"[37] while Watts, exercising a little more panache, suggests that it can be thought of as "intelligent rhythm."[38] *Tao* is usually left untranslated, though it is sometimes referred to as "Way."

The script for the second word of the title, *Te* 德, portrays one acting 彳 with a clear view 罒 of one's heart 心. Often rendered as "power" or "virtue," we translated this term in the *I Ching* as "heart-directed actions."

The word *I* 易 in *I Ching* is a picture of the head 日 and body 勿 of a chameleon 易. As a living organism it symbolizes change in a number of ways. It is able to change its color in relation to its surroundings; its body temperature changes in response to the ambient temperature; and, perhaps most importantly, its life cycle, from birth to death, is marked by continual change: it grows, sheds skin, breathes, and so on.

This book derives an approach to therapy by subsuming therapeutic issues within more general questions about the relational nature of knowing and not-knowing, acting and not-acting. It combs and interweaves ideas from Bateson, Varela, Berry, and others, with concepts drawn from Taoism, and uses the resulting braided notions to articulate what could be called a relational or systemic orientation to therapeutic practice.

According to Bateson, "the basic of rule of systems theory is that, if you want to understand some phenomenon or appearance, you must consider that phenomenon within the context of all *completed* circuits which are relevant to it."[39] A systemic approach to therapy can thus be described in terms of its sensitivity to layered networks of premises and patterns of circular interaction, within and between ideas and people. Some of the various modalities of family therapy could be considered "systemic" within the terms of this definition, particularly those that have explicitly drawn from one or more of the same sources used in this book. The relational orientation notated here, however, makes no attempt to situate itself either within or apart from these other traditions. No apology is offered for either correspondences to, or divergences from, accepted practices of established schools.

The story below is offered as a prelude to what follows. Once told, it, like the questions about family therapy, will be left to echo.

Surly and withdrawn, Alex refused to go to school virtually every day and, if pushed on the issue, would pitch a fit. If his mother did finally manage to get him out the door, his morning would go tolerably well. The grade-six teacher found Alex cooperative and bright, and noted that he got along with his classmates; but it was already late October and he had still made no friends. Alex always came home at noon to eat lunch with his mother, Karen. After the meal, with more school looming before him, he would often throw another tantrum. It was usually effective; he missed a lot of afternoon classes. In the evening, when faced with homework, he would hyperventilate and cry so much that at times his uncle would have to come over to calm him down. The night before Karen called to make an appointment for therapy, Alex told her he no longer wanted to live.

The theme of suicide was familiar to the family. Nine months earlier, with her business bankrupt and marriage of fifteen years crumbling, Karen had taken an overdose of sleeping pills. Her husband, Tim, found her in time to save her life, but it was too late to save the relationship. During her stay in the hospital, she decided she would leave the kids with their father and move in with a friend. But when she was discharged five days later, she came home to find Tim living in their house with another woman. Her outrage galvanized her will and she changed her plans. Taking possession of the two children, she banished her husband from their lives, moved upstate, and secured a new job.

In moving to a new city, Karen hoped to distance herself from the memories and to make a fresh start. But there were problems. The work she found turned sour and she quit. Although she was able to collect unemployment insurance, she felt isolated and depleted. And now, with Alex's tantrums over school and talk of suicide, it wasn't even possible to look for a job, never mind take one. How could she ensure that nothing would happen if she wasn't there to supervise? With Alex becoming harder and harder to handle, Karen began calling Tim, asking for his help in controlling their son. Father, talking to Alex over the phone, could get him to do things—such as go to school—which mother, in person, could not.

As mother and son battled ever more desperately, mother and daughter bonded ever more tightly. Feeling isolated from her adult friends, Karen looked to her eight-year-old daughter, Sandra, for support and companionship. The girl was a model of good manners, and she was doing fine, save for at bedtime. Afraid to sleep alone, Sandra had spent virtually every night since her parents' separation in her mother's bed.

Clearly though, the problem was Alex. If he would obey his mother, go to school, and stop being so depressed and angry, she would be able to find work and get back on her feet. As it was, she felt trapped, sure that the boy would sabotage any move on her part to search for a job. Karen, at her wits' end, wanted help for her son so that he would go to school without a major battle, would make friends, and would start feeling better about himself.

The children's father had told them about their mother's suicide attempt when she was still in the hospital, and although Karen had since discussed it openly and offered reassurances, both children continued to worry about her health, her state of mind, and the potential of her trying again. Alex had been told by friends of the family that he was now the "man" of the house, and he should look out for his mom. Karen dismissed this as inappropriate, insisting that as he was only eleven, he shouldn't be burdened with adult responsibilities. Nevertheless, Alex would lecture her about smoking and complain that he didn't have more say in how their home was run. Despite her problems with him, Karen viewed her son as a sensitive, creative child who was wise beyond his years.

Sensitive and wise. Sensitive, in fact, to his mother's loneliness and feelings of failure, and wise enough to be concerned. Too young to be the responsible "man" his mother told him he didn't have to be, he had found a creative way of looking out for her. In refusing to go to school, in coming home every lunch hour, and in not making friends, he had discovered a way to be with her as much as possible.

In fact, together the children managed to be guardians almost around the clock. Alex took the day shift, while Sandra took care of the night, keeping her mother company through sleepless hours. It was likely that Alex wouldn't make any friends until he was sure that his mother could manage without him. Once he knew, really knew, that she was okay, he would find himself wanting to play with other kids at noon and after school. But right now he believed that his mother needed him at home to help her through this difficult period. Similarly, Sandra would no doubt continue being better behaved than most girls her age, and she would find herself wanting to sleep in her mom's bed for as long as she thought Karen needed her to do this.

One day in November Karen received a call from the government, informing her that they had made an error in allowing her unemployment insurance claim. There was no suggestion of impropriety, but since she had technically not been eligible to receive benefits, she would have to pay back everything she had been given over the last several months. Devastated and lost, she once again considered suicide as a way out.

Four hours later a friend happened to phone her and offer her a job. A month earlier she had turned down a similar opportunity, but this time she took it and started working the next day.

Two weeks later Alex was going to school without a fuss, and he had made some friends. He had started whistling around the house, and he was laughing for the first time in months. Sandra's behavior, on the other hand, had become somewhat annoying. She was complaining about Alex's whistling and had started picking on him.

Over the next months, Karen stopped turning to the children's father for help in resolving disputes. She successfully settled Sandra in her own bed, continued to enjoy and thrive in her job, and began a relationship with a new man. Alex continued to whistle.

There is the matter of the four hours—the time between the first and second phone call, the time when Karen had again thought seriously of suicide. She had phoned her brother and cried and talked to him for quite awhile. And, oh yes, Alex had happened to be home from school that day.

something else, then it too severs: thus absence is also occasioned by presence. Not only "from the first not, a thing is," but also "from the first thing, a not is." Each side of a distinction—for example, assertion/denial, presence/absence, thing/no-thing—creates, and is created by, the other. Each side exists by virtue of the difference that separates it from, and connects it to, its complement. It is the relationship between the two sides that is primary: "The relationship comes first," says Gregory Bateson, "it *precedes*."[1] In the beginning there is the drawing of a distinction, and the knowing of all things (and no-things) is relationally derivative of that simple and primary act.

Francisco Varela considers the making of distinctions to be "one of the most fundamental of all human activities."[2] Bateson, ever fascinated by the ecological life of mind and the mind-full life of ecologies, views distinctions—or, as he would more commonly say, differences—as essential for any characterization of the living world. Inspired by Jung's separation of *creatura* (the living) and *pleroma* (the nonliving), Bateson distinguishes between "the physical world of pleroma, where forces and impacts provide sufficient basis of explanation, and the *creatura*, where nothing can be understood until *differences* and *distinctions* are invoked."[3] Creatura is "the world seen as mind, wherever such a view is appropriate,"[4] and differences are fundamental to its organization. Always in mind there is the distinction, the cut that severs and joins presence and absence.

However, this mind of the living world—that is, the informational processes of perception, communication, learning, evolution, and so on—is a function not only of differences, but also of differences between differences, and differences between these differences between differences: "Every effective difference denotes a demarcation, a line of classification, and all classification is hierarchic. In other words, differences are themselves to be differentiated and classified."[5]

The title of this chapter—"COMPLETION/(CONNECTION/separation)"—notates the manner in which difference differentiates levels of classification; its layered form, described below, will be used as a matrix for exploring how Taoist and systemic thinkers characterize the whole/part relations composing the patterned world of mind. The discussion begins with "separation," moves to the relationship between "separation" and "CONNECTION" and the structure of whole/part complementaries (where the rationale for the use of capitalization and different type sizes will be explained), and concludes with "COMPLETION":

COMPLETION / (CONNECTION/separation)

# separation

I knew that I was a substance whose whole essence or nature is only to think, and which, in order to be, has need of no locus and does not depend on any material thing, in such a way that this self or ego, that is to say, the soul by which I am what I am, is entirely distinct from the body.

—*René Descartes*

It is the attempt to *separate* intellect from emotion that is monstrous, and I suggest it is equally monstrous—and dangerous—to attempt to separate the external mind from the internal. Or to separate mind from body.

—*Gregory Bateson*

When a judgment cannot be framed in terms of good and evil, it is stated in terms of normal and abnormal. And when it is necessary to justify this last distinction, it is done in terms of what is good or bad for the individual. These are expressions that signal the fundamental duality of Western consciousness.

—*Michel Foucault*

As long as there is a dualistic way of looking at things there is no emancipation.

—*Hui-neng*

A distinction marks a boundary which, in Varela's words, "splits the world into two parts, 'that' and 'this,' or 'environment' and 'system,' or 'us' and 'them,' etc."[6] We in the West are steeped in religious, philosophical, scientific, economic, and political traditions whose manifest doctrines and underlying premises embrace an epistemology of separation—from the transcendence of the Judaeo-Christian God, to Plato's absolute division of the intellect and the senses, to the Cartesian cleavage of mind and body and the Newtonian positivist ideal of objectivity, to the exploitation of the environment and the symmetrical posturing of nuclear powers. Many of us also adhere to a mode of chunklike thinking which is best termed *analytic* (from the Greek *ana-*, "throughout," and *lyein*, "to loosen")—confronted with complexity, we break things down into simpler, more manageable constituent parts. Morris Berman characterizes this disjunctive way of knowing as indicative of "nonparticipating consciousness," where

> the knower, or subject "in here," sees himself as radically disparate from the objects he confronts, which he sees as being "out there." In this view, the phenomena of the world remain the same whether or not we are present to observe them, and knowledge is acquired by recognizing a distance between ourselves and nature.[7]

Evidence of this prevailing epistemology can be seen not only *within* traditions and disciplines, but also in the dichotomous separations *between* them. Abraham Maslow describes how both orthodox science and orthodox religion

> have been institutionalized and frozen into a mutually excluding dichotomy. This separation into Aristotelian *a* and *not-a* has been almost perfect, as if a line had been drawn between them in the same way that Spain and Portugal once divided the new world between themselves by drawing a geographical line. Every question, every answer, every method, every jurisdiction, every task has been assigned to either one or the other, with practically no overlaps."[8]

Separation is also inherent in language. To name is to particularize, to define a boundary which distinguishes *this* from *that* which it is not. To name, according to Floyd Merrell,

> is to sort, divide, *differentiate*, order; it is to validate the *differentiating* boundary in which a space is constructed. "Knowledge" derives from the activity of naming and from the possession of names. A boundary cannot be marked off without creating a *difference*, and knowledge is not acquired without marking off boundaries.[9]

The discrete divisions within language—between subject and object, or between static noun and active verb—can seduce us into believing that such separations are not simply the stuff of description, but in fact inhere in the nature of the world. As Benjamin Lee Whorf warns, "we all, unknowingly, project the linguistic relationships of a particular language upon the universe, and *see* them there."[10] Bateson cautions us to beware the human tendency to think and talk as if the world were made up of separable parts:

> All peoples of the world, I believe, certainly all existing peoples, have something like language and, so far as I can understand

the remainder of the personality."[19] Intoxication is thus a kind of subjective "correction of this error,"[20] but as it fades into hangover, the split is only reconfirmed. It should thus be patently evident that it is also mistaken to suppose that technologically inspired crises of the environment are simply in need of technological solutions. Anthony Wilden is very clear: "The conviction that technology will always find an answer is a capital example of the ideological *hubris* which got us into this mess in the first place."[21] Such hubris is an expression of our either/or orientation to the world, a reflection of the assumption that we can *control* nature. Wendell Berry examines the etymology of the word *control*, finding it

> more than ordinarily revealing, . . . for its root meaning is to roll against, in the sense of a little wheel turning in opposition. The principle of control, then, involves necessarily the principle of division: One thing may turn against another thing only by being divided from it. . . .
>
> As we now know, what we turn against must turn against us.[22]

Indeed, echoes Bateson, "*the creature that wins against its environment destroys itself.*"[23]

Such destruction ramifies from the misconstruing and mishandling of distinctions—between subject and object, self and other, humans and environment, mind and body, good and evil, health and sickness, conscious and unconscious, and so on—as pure separations. A chilling example of this can be found in the late Ayatollah Ruhollah Khomeini's pronouncement of the death sentence on author Salman Rushdie and the publishers of *The Satanic Verses*. The killing of the man and the burning of his books will never produce the removal desired by Khomeini, but must virtually guarantee Rushdie's continued presence in Muslim thought and politics.

A distinction *does* create a boundary which divides, but

that self-same boundary simultaneously and irrevocably *connects* that which it separates. Blindness to this simple realization characterizes not only our tragic relationships to each other and our world, but also our relationships to ourselves. Symptoms are haunting reminders that attempts to eradicate pieces of our lived experience, to banish parts of our minds, can unwittingly create and entrench the very problems we most dread. The parted mind does not, indeed cannot, depart.

A man by the name of Martin consulted me for the purpose of getting a retrospective "proper diagnosis." Two years earlier he had gone to see a psychiatrist for what he was afraid might be a "thought disorder." The doctor had seen him for a number of appointments, had listened to his concerns, and had assured him that he wasn't suffering from such an ailment. Martin remained unconvinced: "I know what I feel, what I had. A lot of people will say, my psychiatrist would say, 'You don't have a thought disorder.' But I know what I feel; nobody else does."

This was a difficult stance for the man to take, given his great trust in the expertise of professionals: "To me a psychiatrist knew how a person is supposed to think and knew what a person is supposed to think. . . . A heart doctor knows exactly how the heart works, a psychiatrist knows exactly how the mind works." He would tell his doctor the sorts of thoughts he had, thoughts that, at least for him, were proof that he was somehow "crazy." The mind expert's attempts to reassure him that such thoughts were normal had only served to confirm for Martin that he must then be crazy after all, for it meant that he himself was obviously unable to clearly distinguish what was crazy from what was not:

> MARTIN  When I would go for sessions, as I would talk to
> him, I would walk away thinking, um, like he'd say,
> "Martin, that's not crazy," and I would walk away

thinking—he's in my head now—I would walk away with him thinking in my head [i.e., as if I were the psychiatrist thinking about me]: "If he [Martin] thinks that's crazy, then he's not going to know if jumping off a bridge is crazy, if stabbing somebody's crazy. He won't know what's crazy." And then I became confused and I didn't know, because I was thinking that he was thinking that "he won't know what's crazy anymore." . . . Every time I would go see him I would get worse.

If Martin fashioned the paradoxical knot that bound him in this way, it was his psychiatrist who inadvertently cinched it tight. The Möbius logic that tangled them together went something like this:

THERAPIST He [the psychiatrist] thought that you weren't crazy, but if you thought you were crazy and you weren't, that would mean you wouldn't know the difference between what would be crazy and what wouldn't be crazy, which would mean that you would be crazy.

MARTIN Right, exactly.

And again:

THERAPIST If you said, "Look doctor, I think I have a thought disorder," and he says, "No, you don't have a thought disorder," but if you *think* you have a thought disorder and you don't have a thought disorder, maybe thinking you do have a thought disorder is the thought disorder.

MARTIN Exactly.

Martin's fear of being crazy had not only not been alleviated by the psychiatrist's reassurances, but had been exacerbated. As shall be discussed in detail in chapter 3, a distinc-

tion which makes a difference, which matters, cannot simply
be dissolved; one side cannot be severed from the other. This
man had committed himself to finding out whether or not he
had a thought disorder, and his search, organized by the distinction crazy/not crazy, could not be resolved by the psychiatrist voicing the opinion that one side of the distinction did
not exist; how appropriate, then, that it was the disembodied
voice of the doctor which asserted that it did. The real psychiatrist's voice said the craziness was imagined, and the imagined psychiatrist's voice worried that the craziness was real.

## CONNECTION/separation

The boundary of the organism is *also* the boundary of its environment, and thus its movements can be ascribed to the environment as well. . . . We gain better understanding by describing this boundary and its movements as belonging to both
the organism and its environment.

—*Alan Watts*

Are there any total divisions between things? Is there a place
or time where one thing begins and another ends? If so then
clearly there could be no causal or logical interaction between
them.

—*Gregory Bateson*

If we represent knowledge as a tree, we know that things that
are divided are yet connected. We know that to observe the
divisions and ignore the connections is to destroy the tree.

—*Wendell Berry*

The moment it is acknowledged that distinctions join what
they divide, it becomes impossible to speak of anything in iso-

lation. The implications of this are far-reaching and will continue to cascade throughout this book. For one thing it means that this section cannot be labeled "Connection" and discussed as an independent topic, as it constitutes only one-half of the pair connection/separation. Connection and separation cannot be considered *apart* from each other, but must be considered *a part*[24] of the distinction which, in separating them, connects them.

Varela points out that the classic—what he calls *hegelian*—way of understanding distinctions rests on an assumption of symmetrical opposition and a logic of negation.[25] Taking the form A/not-A, the two sides of a hegelian pair oppose each other at the same logical level: Good is viewed as the opposite of evil, health as the absence of illness, love as the antithesis of hate. Such distinctions are a clear expression of the Western epistemology of separation described earlier: Each side takes on the appearance of atomistic independence, as if it could exist on its own, and does battle with the other.

Varela offers an alternative framework for understanding distinctions that does not negate a hegelian approach (for to do so would simply invoke a hegelian logic of separation at a meta-level: i.e., hegelian/not-hegelian), but rather enfolds it within the layered relationship between wholes and parts.[26] Taking the form

whole / parts constituting the whole

the two sides of this second type of distinction are asymmetrical across hierarchical levels of organization: "Take any situation (domain, process, entity, notion) which is holistic (total, closed, complete, full, stable, self-contained). Put it on the left side of the /. Put on the right side of it the corresponding processes [parts] (constituents, generators, dynamics)."[27] A whole contextualizes the parts it encompasses and is thus of a higher logical type.[28] Or as Bateson would say: "The contrast between part and whole, whenever this contrast appears in the realm of communication, is simply a contrast in logical typing. The whole is always in a metarelationship with its parts."[29] For example, the relational pattern (whole) of a melodic line contextualizes the individual notes that combine to give it form. Varela explains how these levels of whole and part are coemergent:

> Most discussions place holism/reductionism in polar opposition. . . . This seems to stem from the historical split between empirical sciences, viewed as mainly reductionist or analytic, and the (European) schools of philosophy and social science that grope toward a dynamics of totalities. . . . Both attitudes are possible for a given descriptive level, and in fact they are complementary. On the one hand, one can move down a level and study the properties of the components, disregarding their mutual interconnection as a system. On the other hand, one can disregard the detailed structure of the components, treating their behavior only as contributing to that of a larger unit. . . . We cannot conceive of components if there is no system from which they are abstracted; and there cannot be a whole unless there are constitutive elements.[30]

The shape of this whole/part relationship is described by Varela as *imbricated* (overlapping): "A whole decomposes in parts which generate processes integrating the whole."[31] Such mutual creation, "where one term of the pair *emerges* from the other,"[32] can be described as *recursive,* a circular, self-referential process that Heinz von Foerster defines as "turning upon oneself: . . . run[ning] through one's own path again."[33] Bateson, in fact, uses the idea of recursion to distinguish the generation of, and relationship between, levels of informational organization (e.g., of and between wholes and parts) in the domain of creatura:

> It appears that the idea of "logical typing," when transplanted from the abstract realms inhabited by mathematicological phi-

losophers to the hurly-burly of organisms, takes on a very different appearance. Instead of a hierarchy of classes, we face a hierarchy of *orders of recursiveness.*[34]

The self-referential nature of the connection/separation complementarity provides a way of approaching an understanding of such whole/part recursiveness. The reflexivity pivots on the identity between the terms used to describe the function of the slash (/) and those that comprise the distinction itself: that is, the slash *connects and separates connection and separation*—it does what it describes itself doing.[35] This recursive spinning depicts how the difference in levels between wholes and parts is generated: *The connection of* CONNECTION/separation *evolves in the direction of wholeness, while the separation of* CONNECTION/separation *devolves toward a level of particularity.* The capitalization of the left side of the distinction is intended as an analogic reminder that relationships (connections between) contextualize relata (the results of separation), that wholes encompass parts.

The distinction that separates CONNECTION and separation (thereby constituting them as distinct from one another) also connects them (establishes that they are relationally defined). Thus, the distinction (slash) between CONNECTION and separation

    CONNECTION/separation

can itself be distinguished in terms of the two functions it performs; it connects connection and separation—

    CONNECTION OF
        CONNECTION/separation

—and it separates connection and separation:

    separation of
        CONNECTION/separation

These two phrases are each sides of a more encompassing distinction, one that is a higher order of recursion from the first. The change in level is graphically represented by an enlargement in the type size:

(CONNECTION OF
    CONNECTION/separation) /
      (separation of
        CONNECTION/separation)

The divergence between whole and part becomes more and more pronounced as this self-reference is allowed to blossom. The slash between these two parenthetically enclosed terms creates yet another level of contextual complexity, for the processes on either side of *it* can also be connected and separated. Another order of recursion is thus formed:

(CONNECTION OF
    (CONNECTION OF
      CONNECTION/separation) /
        (separation of
          CONNECTION/separation) ) /

    (separation of
      (CONNECTION OF
        CONNECTION/separation) /
        (separation of
          CONNECTION/separation))

And so on.

The reflexive logic of this spiraling of connection/separation can be traced via an analogous distinction—pattern/scatter—within the domain of music. Just as connection/separation folds back, connecting and separating itself, so too the distinction pattern/scatter can be patterned and scattered.

The patterning of PATTERN/scatter—

> PATTERNING OF
>> PATTERN/scatter

—is heard most often in jazz improvisation, where the structure of a familiar tune can serve as the foundational pattern for melodic, harmonic, and rhythmic variations (scatter). Pattern and scatter are continually brought together and interwoven (patterned) in the composition and performance of each piece.

The scattering of PATTERN/scatter—

> scattering of
>> PATTERN/scatter

—differentiates (scatters) two distinct musical forms: (1) the regimented precision (pattern) of, say, marching-band music, where all details of composition and performance are accounted for and strictly defined, and (2) the indeterminate nature (scatter) of aleatory music, where various compositional and/or performance decisions (such as pitch, duration, volume, instrumentation) are made through procedures of random selection (throwing dice, flipping coins, consulting random-number charts, etc.).

The distinction between the patterning and scattering of PATTERN/scatter—

> (PATTERNING OF
>> PATTERN/scatter) /

>> (scattering of
>>> PATTERN/scatter)

—can thus be understood, in musical terms, as:

> (JAZZ IMPROVISATION) /
>> (marching-band music/aleatory music)

Considered at the next level of recursion, the patterning of the previous distinctions—

(PATTERNING OF
    (PATTERNING OF
        PATTERN/scatter) /
      (scattering of
        PATTERN/scatter))

or

(PATTERNING OF
    (JAZZ IMPROVISATION) /
      (marching-band music/aleatory music))

—would combine, in one compositional form, distinct elements of improvisation, determined structure, and randomness. An illustrative, if somewhat eccentric, example of such a combination comes to mind. Imagine a series of marching tunes played and recorded in an exacting manner. A composer might take the audiotape of such a recording, cut it into hundreds of pieces of varying length, and then resplice the sections in random order. This newly, and strangely, edited tape could then be played in a public performance, with a jazz pianist improvising on its indeterminate syncopations.

On the other hand, the scattering of the lower-level distinctions—

(scattering of
    (PATTERNING OF
        PATTERN/scatter) /
      (scattering of
        PATTERN/scatter))

or

(scattering of
    (JAZZ IMPROVISATION) /
      (marching-band music/aleatory music))

—is descriptive of the separate contexts where these musical forms are most often enjoyed. Jazz tends to be found in clubs, marching-band music on football fields and in parades, and aleatory music on college campuses and in concert halls.

Another way of capturing the imbrication of the CON-NECTION/separation relationship is to express it in the form of an injunction:

> (CONNECT SEPARATIONS TO FORM WHOLES) /
> (separate connections to distinguish parts)

The left and right sides of this distinction describe holistic and reductionistic approaches to understanding, respectively. As Varela pointed out above, these two modes of inquiry have been traditionally regarded as dichotomous opposites—an approach to understanding approaches to understanding which is, by virtue of attending only to the separation between the two sides, reductionistic. Varela's alternative—that is, treating holism and reductionism as necessary complements that each have an appropriate and necessary place in the business of knowing[36]—applies the relational principles *within* both traditions to the relationship *between* them. Both are kept separate as unique modalities (a quality derived from reductionism) *and* connected as whole is to part (a derivation of holism):

> (HOLISTICALLY CONNECT
>   HOLISM/reductionism) /
>           (reductionistically separate
>             HOLISM/reductionism)

This is the equivalent of turning the injunction

> (CONNECT SEPARATIONS TO FORM WHOLES) /
> (separate connections to distinguish parts)

back on itself:

(CONNECT
    (CONNECT SEPARATIONS TO FORM WHOLES) /
        (separate connections to distinguish parts)) /

(separate
    (CONNECT SEPARATIONS TO FORM WHOLES) /
        (separate connections to distinguish parts))

The result is the emergence of a kind of *self-referential completion.*

Not all distinctions lend themselves to such reflexive turning, but because in every case the slash necessarily connects and separates the terms on either side of it, *any distinction can be completed by recursively connecting and separating its two terms.* Connecting the separation between A and not-A enables one to move in the direction of wholeness, to a contextual pattern or premise that reflects the nature of the *relationship between* the parts it encompasses, while separating the connection between A and not-A underscores the uniqueness of the *relata* themselves: A is not not-A; not-A is not A.

This process of completion, of embedding the separations of hegelian dualities within the context of the relationship that connects them, can serve as a model for responding to, and participating in the making of, any and all distinctions in the world of communication. With this in mind, the imbricated complementarity

COMPLETION / (CONNECTION/separation)

can now be introduced as a compact rendition of the self-referential spiral generated by the whole/part injunction:

(CONNECT SEPARATIONS TO FORM WHOLES) /
    (separate connections to distinguish parts)

Its tiered form, once explained, will become the principle organizing pattern for the development of ideas in this and subsequent chapters.

The imbrication of

COMPLETION / (CONNECTION/separation)

can be clearly seen when it is recognized that the first-level distinction within the parentheses is repeated at the second level of recursion. Thus,

(CONNECTION/separation)

spirals to become:

COMPLETION / (CONNECTION/separation)

COMPLETION connects CONNECTION/separation, and CON-NECTION/separation separates COMPLETION. The capitalization of COMPLETION distinguishes it as a higher-order connection, the context of connection and separation. It is not a connection that precludes separation, not a holism that opposes reductionism, but a cycling that incorporates both— a unity of "not one, not two,"[37] an expression of the Mahayana Buddhist phrase "Difference is identity; identity is difference."[38]

Thus,

COMPLETION / (CONNECTION/separation)

encapsulates both the first-order distinction,

(CONNECTION/separation)

and its second-order recursion:

(CONNECTION OF CONNECTION/separation) /
    (separation of CONNECTION/separation)

The layered form of COMPLETION / (CONNECTION/ separation) is intended as a matrix for orienting to distinctions, for contextualizing them in terms of the connections of their separations and the separations of their connections. Consider, for instance, the crazy/not crazy difference that organized the relationship between Martin and his psychiatrist. The connection between the two sides of the distinction (metaphorically embodied in the relationship between patient and doctor) was reinforced every time an attempt was made to separate them, to define one as the negation of, or in opposition to, the other. The "thought disorder" thus proved most intractable. Recognizing that the relationship between A and not-A can never be simply an entrenched division, that the separation between them *is* a connection, is the first step toward relating such dichotomies as parts of a context which encompasses them both.

Sanity cannot be achieved by casting out disordered thoughts: As Carl Whitaker likes to remind us, "We are all schizophrenics . . . in the middle of the night when we're sound asleep."[39] The question is not how to successfully sever order and disorder, but how to complete them in such a way that their separation is contextualized by their connection. As any creative artist or scientist could have told the dichotomously distinguished men (patient/psychiatrist) struggling with their dichotomous distinction (crazy/not crazy), the successful *combination* of order and disorder is the essence of creative process. Bateson differentiates "rigor and imagination, the two great contraries of mental process, either of which by itself is lethal. Rigor alone is paralytic death, but imagination alone is insanity."[40]

Mapped onto the model

COMPLETION / (CONNECTION/separation)

this idea can be expressed as

RIGOROUS IMAGINATION /
(ORDERED THOUGHTS / disordered thoughts)

with the lower-case "disordered thoughts" indicative of separation, the small capitals of "ORDERED THOUGHTS" designating a process of connection, and the upper-case "RIGOROUS IMAGINATION" referring to the generative connection of the separation between order and disorder.

The wholeness generated by recursive completions is never conclusive, never a closure, precisely because it is not exclusive of its own decomposition: Completion is a connection that embraces the partitioning of itself. Separation only becomes problematic when it is established as the *context* of relationship, rather than as a subsumed aspect of it—as when, for example, the environment is thought of and treated as *other*. The result of such *alienation* (from the Latin *alis-us*, "other") is expressed in the West as symmetrical confrontation—"the mountain must be conquered"—or as exploitation: "This mountain can be leveled for its timber and its limestone, and the resulting pit will serve as a sterling garbage dump." But the marking of a boundary between self and environment needn't create an epistemological chasm; the distinctiveness of each can be honored when their connection as interactive components in an inclusive ecosystem is underscored. Thus,

COMPLETION / (CONNECTION/separation)

becomes:

ECOSYSTEMIC RELATIONS / (ENVIRONMENT/humans)

Such a pattern illustrates Wendell Berry's contention that "by diminishing nature we diminish ourselves, and vice versa,"[41] and that nature and human culture, wildness and domesticity, are not opposed but are interdependent. Authentic experience of either will reveal the need of one for the other. In fact, examples . . . prove that a human economy and wildness can exist not only in compatibility but to their mutual benefit.[42]

Not all distinctions can be so directly configured, however. The terms *order* and *disorder* respectively describe processes of connection and separation and thus lend themselves naturally to such whole/part stacking; but, if a difference defines a relationship between two *parts,* then the process of transforming them onto the matrix of COMPLETION / (CONNECTION/separation) must include one additional step. Anticipating a discussion later in the chapter, ponder, for illustration, the distinction knower/known.

Both knower and known are "things," abstracted from the relationship of knowing. There is nothing inherent in their relationship that suggests one be thought of as contextually more encompassing than the other, and neither term is necessarily descriptive of a process of either joining (connection) or dividing (separation). In situations such as this—that is, where a distinction marks a relationship between two *parts*—*both* terms are placed on *both* sides of the parenthetically enclosed side of the COMPLETION / (CONNECTION/separation) distinction. That is, knower/known is arrayed on COMPLETION/(CONNECTION/separation) as:

COMPLETION / ((KNOWER/KNOWN) / (knower/known))

These two parenthetical terms can now be treated as distinct descriptions of the relationship between knower and known. The process of knowing is represented as either a connection of knower and known—(KNOWER/KNOWN)—or as a separation between them: (knower/known). The separation of knower and known is characteristic of the Cartesian belief that knowledge is obtained by objectively distancing the observer from the observed; the connection of knower and known, on the other hand, is descriptive of the constructivist belief (to be discussed later) that the knower is implicated in the known, that there is no separation between them:

COMPLETION /
((CONNECTED, CONSTRUCTIVIST KNOWING) /
(disjunctive, cartesian knowing))

Completing the distinction between these two orientations ensures that they not be dichotomized, but rather contextually enfolded within an approach to knowing that is inclusive of them both:

CONTEXTUAL KNOWING /
(CONNECTED KNOWING / separated knowing)

The separation of knower and known needn't remain separate from the connection of knower and known, as Wendell Berry's poem "The Cold" relates:

How exactly good it is
to know myself
in the solitude of winter,

my body containing its own
warmth, divided from all
by the cold; and to go

separate and sure
among the trees cleanly
divided, thinking of you

perfect too in your solitude,
your life withdrawn into
your own keeping

—to be clear, poised
in perfect self-suspension
toward you, as though frozen.

And having known fully the
goodness of that, it will be
good also to melt.[43]

To reiterate: The spirial matrix COMPLETION / (CONNEC-
TION/separation) can be used to take the two sides of any given
distinction—whether whole/part or part/part—and to consider ways in which they mutually define, propose, create, and/
or maintain one another in an encompassing pattern of interaction. Whole/part distinctions—such as context/text, envi-
ronment/species, melody/note—or those that are descriptive
of processes of connection/separation—such as integrate/dis-
integrate, information/noise, gather/scatter—can be mapped
directly onto the right side of the pattern:

COMPLETION / (CONTEXT/text)
COMPLETION / (ENVIRONMENT/species)
COMPLETION / (MELODY/note)
COMPLETION / (INTEGRATE/dis-integrate)
COMPLETION / (INFORMATION/noise)
COMPLETION / (GATHER/scatter)

Part/part distinctions—such as front/back, presence/absence,
sound/silence, warp/woof—are doubly placed on the right
side of the larger distinction, in order that a CONNECTION/sep-
aration relationship can be created:

COMPLETION / ((FRONT/BACK) / (front/back))
COMPLETION / ((PRESENCE/ABSENCE) / (presence/absence))
COMPLETION / ((SOUND/SILENCE) / (sound/silence))
COMPLETION / ((WARP/WOOF) / (warp/woof))

In all cases, the far left side of each tiered relation can be considered a context or completion: a connection of connection and separation.

# COMPLETION /
## (CONNECTION/separation)

A Mind Poet
Stays in the house.
The house is empty
And it has no walls.
The poem
Is seen from all sides,
Everywhere,
At once.

*—Gary Snyder*

The matrix COMPLETION / (CONNECTION/separation) will now be used as a pattern with which to encounter the textured grain of Taoism, systemic thought, and the practice of therapy. In this process it will produce moiré phenomena— forms created by the rhythmic interface of patterns[44]—which will be both related and distinct from their sources. As these interactive patterns are then brought to bear upon one another, multilevel moirés can be expected to develop, providing the sorts of double or multiple descriptions which Bateson considers necessary for an in-depth view and understanding.[45] Such contrapuntal weaving can be understood as an exercise in what Bateson terms *abduction,* that is, "the lateral extension of abstract components of description." Abduction is a necessary attribute of all mind-full activities: "Metaphor, dream, parable, allegory, the whole of art, the whole of science, the whole of religion . . . are instances or aggregates of instances of abduction."[46]

The first moiré to emerge derives from an initial exploration of Taoism; however, the shape of this pattern will very soon thereafter be used to broach Bateson's notions of Mind. A circling between these two domains of thought will then ensue, giving rise to issues regarding the relationship between the nature of mind and the Mind of Nature.

## TAO / ((YIN/YANG) / (yin/yang))

| | |
|---|---|
| STUDENT | Where is Tao? |
| TEACHER | Right before us. |
| STUDENT | Why don't I see it? |
| TEACHER | Because of your egoism you cannot see it. |
| STUDENT | If I cannot see it because of my egoism, does your Reverence see it? |
| TEACHER | As long as there is "I and thou," this complicates the situation and there is no seeing Tao. |
| STUDENT | When there is neither "I" nor "thou" is it seen? |
| TEACHER | When there is neither "I" nor "thou," who is here to see it? |

—*Yen-kuan Ch'i-an*

The Taoists never dichotomized their contraries (i.e., they conceived of them as YIN/YANG rather than yin/yang). As the *T'ai Chi* ("grand" 太 "polarity" 極) symbol elegantly portrays, the shaded side (yin 陰) of the circle is dark only to the extent that the light side (yang 陽) is bright; the boundary they share exists by virtue of their relationship, and each "side" contains within it the seed of the other (see figure 1). This creates a continually moving, circling balance wherein one side of the distinction is always proposing the existence of the other.

Figure 1. The T'ai Chi Symbol

The archaic form of the Chinese character *yin* 👆 is a picture of clouds, while the ancient form of *yang* 👆 depicts the sun ☉ shining 👆 from above the horizon —. Each has qualities or attributes associated with it, but only in relation to its complement. Thus, for example, yin withdraws inward and down as yang moves outward and up; yin is empty in relation to yang's fullness, yin is soft to the extent that yang is hard, and so on. The emphasis is always on the recursive balance created by their mutual definition, as can be seen in the following passage from chapter 2 of Lao Tzu's *Tao Te Ching*:

> Presence and absence reciprocally grow
> Difficult and easy reciprocally complete
> Long and short reciprocally shape
> High and low reciprocally contrast
> Sound and notes reciprocally harmonize
> Back and front reciprocally follow.[47]

Where is the Tao in all of this? Abductively extrapolating from the pattern

TAO / ((YIN/YANG) / (yin/yang))

we will be poised to look for it in the *reciprocal relationship between* the connection and separation of yin and yang, in the circuitous way their twoness is one and their oneness is two. Front can follow back only if they are cyclically connected, and indeed Lao Tzu does make reference to the Tao in terms of circular motion:

反 者 道 之 動

"Returning: Tao's moving[48]

Tao is not a thing, or a conglomerate of parts, but a process of recursive relationship, emergent from the connected separation of yin and yang. The imbricated complementarity of Taoism—TAO / ((YIN/YANG) / (yin/yang))—is not so much a body of ideas to be learned as an orientation to knowing and not knowing, a continual reminder to connect one's separations and separate one's connections in recursive ways. The Tao is inclusive of, and dependent on, the distinction yin/yang as a necessary part of its wholeness.

The poet Lionel Kearns manages to convey something of this self-referentiality in his visual poem "The Birth of God" (see figure 2).[49] The gestalt of the whole is different from, yet derivative of, the layered crossover of the parts. It all happens in the relations between.

Layered complementarities provide an avenue for approaching what Bateson refers to as *Mind*. He considers "mental function" to be immanent in the interaction of differentiated parts,[50] that is, "in the ensemble as a *whole*."[51] Wholes are constituted by the combined interaction of the parts,[52] and this interaction is circular: the simplest unit of mind is "the elementary cybernetic system with its messages in circuit."[53] Expressed in spiral form, Mind thus becomes:

MIND /

    (CIRCUITOUS INTERACTION BETWEEN PARTS /

      differentiation of parts)

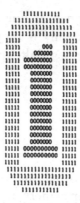

Figure 2. The Birth of God

As we shall see, there is a resonance between Tao and Mind, an abductive relationship that recalls Watts's analysis of the etymology of Tao as "intelligent rhythm."[54] The Tao's rhythmic (patterned)—and immanent (relational)—nature is suggested in chapter 5 of the *Tao Te Ching*, where Lao Tzu likens it, by implication, to the action of a bellows:

> Between Heaven and Earth,
> There seems to be a Bellows:
> It is empty, and yet it is inexhaustible;
> The more it works, the more comes out of it.
> No amount of words can fathom it:
> Better look for it within you.[55]

Chang explains that

> the understanding of *Tao* is an inner experience in which distinction between subject and object vanishes. It is an intuitive, immediate awareness rather than a mediated, inferential, or intellectual process. *Tao* does not blossom into vital consciousness until all distinctions between self and nonself have disappeared.[56]

The immanence of Tao makes it possible to look for it within;[57] however, it also demands the converse search—that is, to follow it (as Mind) as it extends outward, beyond the confines of our "skin encapsulated ego"[58] to its encompassment in the ecosystemic relations of which we are a part. In the words of Bateson:

> The individual mind is immanent but not only in the body. It is immanent also in pathways and messages outside the body; and there is a larger Mind of which the individual mind is only a subsystem. This larger Mind is comparable to God and is perhaps what some people mean by "God," but it is still immanent in the total interconnected social system and planetary ecology.[59]

This embedding of mind within Mind—like Chinese box within Chinese box—is also apparent in the work of Varela, who uses the metaphor of "conversation" to talk about the recursive layering of parts and whole:

> There is a sense in which we must consider individual organisms and their (internal) cognitive processes. However, it is equally true . . . to realize that cognitive processes can also be seen as operating at the *next higher level,* that is, the cognitive processes of the autonomous unit of which *we* are participants and components. . . . To this next higher level belong the characteristics of mind we attribute to ourselves individually; in fact, what we experience as our mind cannot truly be separated from this network to which we connect and through which we interdepend. . . .
>
> From this point of view, then, mind is an immanent quality, of a class of organizations including individual living systems, but also ecological aggregates, social units of various sorts, brains, conversations, and many others, however spatially distributed or short-lived. There is mind in every unity engaged in conversationlike interactions.[60]

Given such a conception of Mind, what then is *knowing*? In order to find an appropriately relational answer, it will help to orient our inquiry in relational terms. A template can be found in Warren McCulloch's famous double question: "What is a number, that a man may know it, and a man, that he may know a number?"[61] Asked of the relationship between knower and known, the query becomes: What is the known that a knower may know it, and what is a knower that it may know a known?

# KNOWING /
## ((KNOWER/KNOWN) / (knower/known))

We subtract or repress our awareness that perception is active and repress our awareness that action is passive.
— *Gregory Bateson*

Mind is immanent in "the pattern which connects all the living creatures";[62] it is a pattern of patterns "which defines the vast generalization that, indeed, it is patterns which connect."[63] This assertion aptly illustrates the fine line Bateson treads between the concerns of ontology—"problems of how things are, what is a person, and what sort of a world this is"[64]—and issues of epistemology—"how we know anything, or more specifically, how we know what sort of a world it is and what sort of creatures we are that can know something (or perhaps nothing) of this matter."[65]

Alasdair MacIntyre credits Christian Wolff (1679–1754) with canonizing *ontologia* as a philosophical term. Wolff "argued a priori that the world is composed of simple substances, themselves neither perceived nor possessing extension or shape."[66] Thus, ontology has to do with "being," with how things "really" are, independent of an observer. Ontologically speaking, knower and known are distinct entities (i.e., the relationship between them is one of knower/known rather than KNOWER/KNOWN); both maintain an existence and identity before, during, and after taking part in the particular activity of knowing that brings them together. From an epistemological standpoint, the connection between knower and known (i.e., KNOWER/KNOWN) bestows existence upon the known. However, Gregory Bateson and Mary Catherine Bateson argue that "because what *is* is identical for all human purposes with what can be known, there can be no clear line between epistemology and ontology."[67] In other words, because the known world is a world of knowing, ontology is subsumed within epistemology: KNOWING / (EPISTEMOLOGY/ontology). Bateson insists that the definition of a reality is dependent upon an observer doing the defining, imposing a meaning: "Bishop Berkeley was right, at least in asserting that what happens in the forest is *meaningless* if he is not there to be affected by it."[68] Further, he reminds us that "'parts,' 'wholes,' 'trees,' and 'sounds' exist as such only in quotation marks. It is *we* who differentiate 'tree' from 'air' and 'earth,' 'whole' from 'part,' and so on."[69]

In this, Bateson is in accord with the Heisenberg transformations taking place in a variety of disciplines.[70] Alan Watts relates that "from physics to psychology, every department of science is realizing more and more that to observe the world is to participate in it, and that, frustrating as this may first seem to be, it is the most important clue of all to further knowledge."[71] Morris Berman captures it most eloquently: "We are sensuous participants in the very world we seek to describe."[72] In a word, we *construct* reality.

The foundation of such a participatory world is not lost in the ephemeral instability of solipsistic hallucination, nor found in the supposed stability of an ontologically distinct reality. Rather, as Varela indicates, it is grounded in *experience,* in the relationship of knowing:

> It should now be clear that the first cut, the most elementary distinction we can make, may be the intuitively satisfactory cut between oneself *qua* experiencing subject on the one side, and one's experience on the other. But this cut can under no circumstances be a cut between oneself and an independently existing world of objective objects. Our "knowlege," whatever rational meaning we give that term, must begin with experience, and with cuts *within* our experience—such as, for instance, the cut we make between the part of our experience that we come to call "ourself" and all the rest of our experience, which we then call our "world." Hence, this world of ours, no matter how we structure it, no matter how well we manage to keep it stable with permanent objects and recurrent interactions, is by definition a world codependent with our experience, and not the ontological reality of which philosophers and scientists alike have dreamed.[73]

As the left side of the imbricated complementarity

CONSTRUCTED EXPERIENCE /

((KNOWER/KNOWN) / (knower/known))

the notion of CONSTRUCTED EXPERIENCE accounts for the connection between the connection and separation of knower and known. The ontological splitting of knower and known—knower/known—is itself an epistemological act. The separation of knower and known is not, in this sense, objectively real, but rather a necessary and helpful distinction drawn within the context of an epistemological connection (i.e., within the context of KNOWER/KNOWN).

Formalized as a philosophical stance, such a constructivist view focuses concern on the implications and ethics of connected knowing, thus bridging the schism separating the equally dichotomous epistemologies of solipsism and naive realism:

KNOWING / ((CONSTRUCTIVISM) / (subjectivism/objectivism))

Ernst von Glasersfeld, a leading proponent of constructivist thinking, explains that

> radical constructivism . . . is radical because it breaks with convention and develops a theory of knowledge in which knowledge does not reflect an "objective" ontological reality, but exclusively an ordering and organization of a world constituted by our experience. The radical constructivist has relinquished "metaphysical realism" once and for all and finds himself in full agreement with Piaget, who says, "Intelligence organizes the world by organizing itself." [74]

Bateson does not limit such intelligence (mind) to the strictly human, and thus he makes what sound to be ontological statements about the knowing of other members of Creatura. He will assert that a tree exists only in quotation marks, but will then also maintain that this quotationed biological form is involved in its *own* knowing, its own constructions: "Do not forget that the 'tree' is alive and therefore itself capable of receiving certain sorts of information. It too may discriminate 'wet' from 'dry.'" [75] And when the tree dies and falls, it becomes part of the knowing of the forest: "Bishop Berkeley always forgot the grass and the squirrels in the woods, for whom the falling tree made a *meaningful* sound" [76]—or, if not a sound, at least a meaningful difference.

If Bateson is right, the tree will not know how to recognize "moisture" per se, but rather the *difference between* moisture and the lack thereof: "All receipt of information is necessarily the receipt of news of *difference,* and all perception of difference is limited by threshold. Differences that are too slight or too slowly presented are not perceivable."[77] Bateson's *difference,* like Spencer-Brown's *distinction,*[78] proposes *relationship* as the fundamental building block of Mind. However, a "building block" metaphor is inappropriate, for it implies the foundation is solid. Such permanence is not possible, given that a difference is not a concrete thing with dimensions in space and time—it is a relationship in mind, and mind, says Bateson, "is empty; it is no-thing. It exists only in its ideas, and these again are no-things."[79]

Ideas (and here we return to the notion of circular process) are, according to Bateson, the transforms of difference traveling in a circuit;[80] the whole of Mind, then, from difference on up, is change upon change upon recursive change:

> Our sensory system—and surely the sensory systems of all other creatures (even plants?) and the mental systems behind the senses (i.e., those parts of the mental systems inside the creatures)—can only operate with *events* which we can call *changes.*[81]

Varela concludes:

> All of this boils down, actually, to a realization that although the world *does* look solid and regular, when we come to examine it there is no fixed point of reference to which it can be pinned down; it is nowhere substantial or solid. The whole of experience reveals the co-dependent and relative quality of all knowledge.[82]

And yet, are these statements about the impossibility of ontology not ontological in form? Is the assertion about there being no fixed point of reference not itself such a point? If it is, then it self-referentially proves itself wrong; and if it isn't, then clearly fixed points of reference *are* possible and again it is wrong. Such paradoxes are comfortably familiar to Taoists, who welcome them into the fabric of their thought, and we shall be examining some of these shortly. Suffice it to say at this point that such oscillations need never, and can never, be contained. As soon as the knower is figured into his or her knowing, there will be self-reference; in fact, there would be no "self," no conscious mind without it. Consciousness is defined by Bateson and Bateson as "a reflexive aspect of mental process that occurs in some but not all minds, in which the knower is aware of some fraction of his knowledge or the thinker of some fraction of his thought."[83]

The paradox of ontologically denying ontology can be mapped as part of

EXPERIENCE /
((EPISTEMOLOGY/ONTOLOGY)/(epistemology/ontology))

where any definitive statement about the epistemological nature of knowing necessarily becomes an ontological assertion of "the way things really are." A denial of ontology is an assertion of the dichotomous split—(epistemology/ontology)—between the two. But as has been said many times, the act of separating is itself a connection; in making the assertion of the denial, the denied is asserted, and the connection between the two—(EPISTEMOLOGY/ONTOLOGY)—is forged.

This need not be marked as a problem to be eschewed, but can be welcomed as a *koan* to be chewed.[84] If knowing begins in relationship, then ontological statements are always properly contextualized as a part of experience, not apart from it as an ontology, left to its own devices, would insist. Conversely, epistemological statements can never be taken as assertions about some kind of internalized knowing. Experience is relational and knowing is circular—there is no settled place from which to start or for which to head. Varela constructs an orientation we might term "not inside, not outside":[85]

EXPERIENCE /
  ((INSIDE/OUTSIDE) / (inside/outside))

Reality is not just constructed at our whim, for that would be to assume that there is a starting point we can choose from: inside first. It also shows that reality cannot be understood as given and that we are to perceive it and pick it up, as a recipient, for that would also be to assume a starting point: outside first. . . .

  [This] reveals to us a world where "no-ground," "no-foundation" can become the basis of understanding.[86]

The pattern EXPERIENCE / (EPISTEMOLOGY/ontology) also surfaces in Bateson's work in a slightly altered form— EPISTEMOLOGY / (EPISTEMOLOGY/ontology)—as an attempt to describe relationally, at many different levels, the knowing, the epistemology, of Creatura. That is, he begins with an ontological assertion that all minds have their own local epistemologies, their own ways of participating in the patterning of differences (as in the knowing of trees and grass). But he then goes on to assume that these patterns are subsumed in a pattern which connects them in an inclusive epistemology of Mind.[87] This whole/part stacking of knowing gives form to a layered version of the McCulloch question: What is Mind that a mind may know it, and a mind that it may know Mind?

  Or can Mind be known? Can the part know the whole? Spencer-Brown characterizes the situation this way:

We cannot escape the fact that the world we know is constructed in order (and thus in such a way as to be able) to see itself. . . .

This indeed is amazing. . . .

But *in order* to do so, evidently it must first cut itself up into at least one state which sees, and at least one other state which is seen. In this severed and mutilated condition, whatever it sees is *only partially* itself. We may take it that the world undoubtedly is itself (i.e., is indistinct from itself), but, in any attempt to see itself as an object, it must, equally undoubtedly, act so as to make itself distinct from, and therefore false to, itself. In this condition it will always partially elude itself.[88]

Our double question must thus become: What is the knowing of mind that it cannot know the knowing of Mind, and the knowing of Mind that it cannot be known by the knowing of mind? Bateson sheds further light:

If, as we must believe, the total mind is an integrated network (of propositions, images, processes, neural pathology, or what have you—according to what scientific language you prefer to use), and if the content of consciousness is only a sampling of different parts and localities in this network; then, inevitably, the conscious view of the network as a whole is a monstrous denial of the *integration* of that whole. From the cutting of consciousness, what appears above the surface is *arcs* of circuits instead of either the complete circuits or the larger complete circuits of circuits.[89]

We are, in part, constrained by language with its cursed pleromatic touch. How can one characterize the relational Mind of Creatura when everything language touches is turned into a "thing"? Bateson and Bateson lament:

If it is true that there are *things* in Pleroma, then nouns (which are not things) are a useful invention for thinking about things —but with nouns we have invented the capacity for false reification. There are no things in Creatura—only ideas, images, clusters of abstract relations—but the vast convenience of talking about things leads us to treat any available idea—truth, God, charisma—as if it were thing-like.[90]

This peculiarity of language is not newly recognized; 2,500 years ago Lao Tzu introduced the *Tao Te Ching* with this *caveat orator* (let the speaker beware!):

道 可 道 非 常 道

The Tao that can be told of is not the eternal Tao.[91]

It seems there are places where language, perception, and knowing cannot, and perhaps should not, reach if wholeness is to be protected. Bateson clarifies the constraints: "There is always, of course, violence to the whole system if you think about the parts separately; but we're going to do that if we want to think at all, because it's too difficult to think about everything at once."[92] Confronted with such impossibility, the challenge is to construct an imaginative and playful response. Lao Tzu is a wonderful exemplar in this regard.

## TAO / (KNOWING/not-knowing)

Emptiness constantly falls within our reach; it is always with us and in us, and conditions all our knowledge, all our deeds, and is our life itself. It is only when we attempt to pick it up and hold it forth as something before our eyes that it eludes us, frustrates all our efforts, and vanishes like vapour.

—D. T. Suzuki

After telling us that "the Tao that can be told of is not the eternal Tao," Lao Tzu continues with a parallel phrase, again comprised of six characters. Wing-Tsit Chan's translation reads:

名 可 名 非 常 名

The name that can be named is not the eternal name.[93]

Once caught in language Tao is bound, and its identity is predicated on its being distinct from that which it is not—against which it can stand in relief. However, there is nothing that is not Tao; because it is already complete, there is no necessity for an other-than-Tao to complement it. Tao is not an "it," but an inclusive unity, a process that encompasses its own absence. Thus, for Tao to remain integral, to not be cleft by the distinctions and differences of thought and perception, it must remain unnamed 無 名,[94] as well as unseen 不 見, unheard 不 聞, and ungrasped 不 得.[95]

Uncaptured in language, Tao remains unknown: As was explained earlier, this is not a separation of transcendence, but of necessity. As Bateson recognizes, "Those distinctions that remain undrawn are *not*."[96] By not being distinguished, by remaining *not*, the Tao stays whole. Rather than being split in two—a Tao and an other-than-Tao—it embraces its otherness by not being differentiated from it in the first place.

Or is that true? Can Tao *not* not be whole? Deny it or not, Tao *is* named—it is Tao. Can it then not fail to not be whole? Is it possible to snatch the name away after the fact—that is, can a distinction, once drawn, be undrawn?[97] But without naming it in the first place there could be no Tao to not name. At issue are the threats to the holiness and health of wholeness[98] when confronted in language by a knowing that is partial and partialing. Like plucking a budding flower to understand the beauty of its developing form and contextual fit, subjecting the Tao to scrutiny can isolate and kill it. "It is very difficult," Bateson remarks,

> to talk about those living systems that are healthy and doing well; it's much easier to talk about living matters when they are sick, when they're disturbed, when things are going wrong. Pathology is a relatively easy thing to discuss, health is very difficult. This, of course, is one of the reasons why there is such a thing as the sacred, and why the sacred is difficult to talk about, because the sacred is peculiarly related to the healthy. One does not like to disturb the sacred, for in general, to talk about something changes it, and perhaps will turn it into a pathology.[99]

If language falters when approaching the sacred ground of wholeness, how can the *Tao Te Ching* fail to fail at speaking the unspeakable, fail to pathologize the Tao? How do we reconcile Lao Tzu's five-thousand-word exposition on something that should not—indeed cannot—be exposed? The ninth-century Tang poet P'o Chü-i clearly had this in mind when he teased:

> Those who speak do not know
> Those who know do not speak—
> So says Lao Tzu
> If Lao Tzu is a knower
> Why did he write 5000 words?[100]

Why indeed. Would it not have been more Taoist to not have written a word? After all:

> Good walking leaves no track behind it;
> Good speech leaves no mark to be picked at.[101]

But Lao Tzu is advocating something different here than not walking or not speaking in the first place. Rather, he suggests the possibility of not getting imprisoned in the distinctions we must inevitably draw. Bateson reminds us that "of necessity we shall split our descriptions when we talk about the universe. But there may be better and worse ways of doing this splitting of the universe into nameable parts."[102] And there may be better and worse ways of gathering the parts into forms of expression; perhaps there are ways of adapting the limitations of language as resources for saying what can't be said.

Despite inevitable whole/part separations, Bateson does locate opportunities for resonance between the Mind of Creatura and the expression of mind in language, and this opens the possibility for shaping our descriptions to accord with the patterned ways in which Creatura describes itself to itself. The bridge lies in those aspects of language and thought that themselves are fundamentally relational—metaphor and story. Metaphor is not simply a literary form; it "runs right through Creatura"[103] and is thus "right at the bottom of being alive."[104]

The biological world, organized relationally, is metaphorically composed: the petals and sepals of a flower are metaphors of leaves; the elephant's trunk is a metaphor of the human nose; the wombat, a marsupial, is a metaphor of the mammalian woodchuck; and so on. The metaphor of metaphor is a way of addressing the connected separation of biological forms, the pattern of their corresponding distinctiveness. Octavio Paz explains how metaphor maintains the integrity of "not one, not two":

> Analogy is the science of correspondences. It is, however, a science which exists only by virtue of differences. Precisely because this is not that, it is possible to extend a bridge between this and that. The bridge is the word like, or the word is: this is like that, this is that. The bridge does not do away with distance: it is an intermediary; neither does it eliminate differences: it establishes a relation between different terms. . . . Analogy says that everything is the metaphor of something else.[105]

Bateson defines *story* as "an aggregate of formal relations scattered in time to make a sequence having a certain sort of minuet formal dance to it." [106] In the connections between characters, in the development of plot and the time of its telling, it weaves a pattern. Story and thought are one and the same.

> [This] is in fact how people think, and it is . . . the only way in which they could think. There are no other ways of dealing with this problem of relations in a succinct form in which all the relations you want to think about sort of simultaneously can get into the picture together or get into the picture piled on top of each other so they pull on each other the right way. This is the function of stories. . . . What is true is the relations within the story. [107]

William Carlos Williams adds a layer of self-referential grace to the expression of this relational view by gathering mind and poem together in a poem mindful of itself. [108]

Be patient that I address you in a poem,
        there is no other
                fit medium.
The mind
        lives there. It is uncertain,
            can trick us and leave us
agonized. But for resources
        what can equal it?
            There is nothing. We
should be lost
        without its wings to
            fly off upon.
. . . . . . . . . . . . . . . . . . . . . . . . .
   A new world
      is only a new mind.
           And the mind and the poem
are all apiece. [109]

The story, as Bateson tells it, is not unique to human thought, but rather joins our mind with the Mind of Creatura:

> The fact of thinking in terms of stories does not isolate human beings as something separate from the starfish and the sea anemones, the coconut palms and the primroses. Rather, if the world be connected, if I am at all fundamentally right in what I am saying, then *thinking in terms of stories* must be shared by all mind or minds, whether ours or those of redwood forests and sea anemones.[110]

This opens the possibility of modeling our storied descriptions on the organization of the living stories described: "A scientist describing an earthworm might start at the head end and work down its length—thus producing a description iconic in its sequence and elongation."[111] In the same spirit, Bateson praises the poet (and botanist) Goethe[112] for straightening out

> the gross comparative anatomy of flowering plants. He discovered that a "leaf" is not satisfactorily defined as "a flat green thing" or a "stem" as "a cylindrical thing." The way to go about the definition—and undoubtedly somewhere deep in the growth processes of the plant, this is how the matter is handled—is to note that buds (i.e., baby stems) form in the angles of leaves. From that, the botanist constructs the definitions on the basis of the relations between stem, leaf, bud, angle, and so on.
> "*A stem is that which bears leaves.*"
> "*A leaf is that which has a bud in its angle.*"
> "*A stem is what was once a bud in that position.*"[113]

Thus, the biologist's descriptions have the potential for some sort of valid "fit," in that they

> may follow the classification of parts and relations which the DNA and/or other biological systems of control themselves

use. . . . In any case, [the biologist] has the possibility of being right in a sense the physicist can never achieve.[114]

We see here the ontological edge of Bateson's epistemological knife, and why he would consider himself "almost a positivist."[115] If this be positivism, it is at least of a biological variety, and, informed by the metaphorical notion that mind is synecdochical of Mind, it pays heed to the gaps. Knowing subjected to knowing will never be represented and never be whole; the most that can be achieved is a moiré pattern reflective of the encounter and an appreciation for what must be left unspoken. William Carlos Williams:

> How shall we get said what must be said?
>
> Only the poem.
> . . . . . . . . . . . .
>                     Only the poem
> only the made poem, to get said what must
> be said, not to copy nature, sticks
> in our throats    .[116]

Were Bateson working purely within a positivist tradition, he would view such gaps in knowledge and description—what sticks in the throat—as temporary potholes to be filled in and paved over as soon as possible. This is clearly not the case. He, like the Taoists, recognizes that one who approaches Mind or Tao in this way—rushing after it, striving diligently forward and attempting to learn more and more—will inevitably come up empty-handed. An empty hand is, however, a fine place to start. Lao Tzu advises:

> fussing spoils
> grasping loses
> The Sage doesn't fuss—thus doesn't spoil
>          doesn't grasp—thus doesn't lose[117]

Since Tao is empty 虛,[118] there is nothing to grasp; and like an empty bowl 用, it can never 不 be brimmed 盈:[119]

> Practicing learning: daily accumulating
> Practicing Tao: daily diminishing [120]

Poets and Taoists alike honor what sticks in the throat, what can't be said: "There are many matters and many circumstances in which *consciousness* is undesirable and silence is golden," Bateson and Bateson advise, "so that secrecy can be used as a *marker* to tell us that we are approaching holy ground." [121] Words fill; in silence the emptiness of Tao remains pristine. The Zen poet Ryota whispers:

> They spoke no word.
> The visitor, the host
> And the white chrysanthemum.[122]

But for silence to be silence, sound must be in the air. Each is a request for the other, as John Cage so eloquently says (and, in the gaps, doesn't-say) in his "Lecture on Nothing": [123]

```
I am here              ,      and there is nothing to say          .
                                                If among you are
those who wish to get somewhere      ,        let them leave at
any moment        .                What we re-quire              is
silence          ;          but what silence requires
          is        that I go on talking  .
[ . . . . . . . . ]
                                                                But
now                          there are silences              and the
words              make              help make                   the
silences              .
                                        I have nothing to say
          and I am saying it                              and that is
poetry                          as I need it                    .
```

There is no getting away from the schisms of language, perception, and knowing. And, in fact, no need to. The point is to not get caught inside the distinctions we create, and that won't happen as long as our separations are connected and our connections can be separated: There is always a way out. Of course the way *out* will always simultaneously be a way *inside* another boundary. Freedom from limitation is not an escape from distinctions—that would only be death—but a playful movement between, a continual oscillation between, connection and separation. If Taoism were only connection it would not exist; as Varela attests, there must be whole *and* parts:

> There is a strong current in contemporary culture advocating autonomy, information (symbolic descriptions), and holism as some sort of cure-all and as a radically "new" dimension. This is often seen in discussions about environmental phenomena, human health, and management. . . . We take a rather different view. We simply see autonomy and control, causal and symbolic explanations, reductionism and holism as complementary or "cognitively adjoint" for the understanding of those systems in which we are interested. They are intertwined in any satisfactory description; each entails some loss relative to our cognitive preferences, as well as some gain.[124]

Cage's talking about nothing is a way of not-talking about the something of emptiness; much gets said in the spaces between. Let us take another look at the first line of the *Tao Te Ching*, at how Lao Tzu uses a poetic sensibility to not-say what needs saying; he employs what we might call a strategy of con-volution. Chan's rendition of the line—"The Tao that can be told of is not the eternal Tao"[125]—does not make clear the threefold repetition of the word *Tao* in the original Chinese. Word for word it reads:

道 可 道 非 常 道

Tao able to Tao not forever[126] Tao

The second *Tao* can be partially retained in translation by embedding it within a pun: "Tao endowed is not forever Tao."[127] The Tao that is able to be endowed with attributes is not the Tao of pure ongoing process. And yet the word *forever*, used to describe the nature of the "real" Tao, functions in the sentence as an adjective—it is an attribute. Thus the sentence affirms and denies itself in continual oscillation. The Möbius pattern can be depicted as:

TAO /
    ((FOREVER TAO / ENDOWED TAO) /
      (endowed Tao / forever Tao))

The denial of the connection (i.e., the separation) between the endowed Tao and the forever Tao—"Endowed Tao not forever Tao"—is depicted by the enclosed distinction on the far right—(endowed Tao / forever Tao). The denial of the denial (i.e., the connection)—that the forever Tao is *not* not endowed—is shown by the distinction (FOREVER TAO / ENDOWED TAO). The Tao reflexively completes these two terms.

It is this, the oscillation, that speaks to both the presence and absence of the Tao in a way in which the words written as technical prose—that is, where all attention is directed toward describing the presence of what is, without the necessary self-consciousness to not-say what is not—could not. The endless turning generated by the internal paradox of the sentence is analogous to the recursive, empty process of the Tao.

The separations between the thought and the unthinkable reflect the necessary disjunction between whole and part, and a respect for not-knowing is a respect for the integrity of what Wendell Berry calls *mystery:*

> To call the unknown by its right name, "mystery," is to suggest that we had better respect the possibility of a larger, unseen pattern that can be damaged or destroyed and, with it, the smaller patterns. . . .
>
> If we are up against mystery, then we dare act only on the most modest assumptions. The modern scientific program has held that we must act on the basis of knowledge, which, because its effects are so manifestly large, we have assumed to be ample. But if we are up against mystery, then knowledge is relatively small, and the ancient program is the right one: Act on the basis of ignorance. Acting on the basis of ignorance, paradoxically, requires one to know things, remember things—for instance, that failure is possible, that error is possible, that second chances are desirable.[128]

As a variation of the imbricated complementarity COMPLE-TION / (CONNECTION/separation), Berry's position can be presented as MYSTERY / (RESPECT/ignorance), where the connection between respect (a sign of connection to the whole) and ignorance (a recognition of necessary separation from the whole) becomes a guide for action.

The informative loop between the limits of knowing and the ethics of acting is also found in constructivist circles, where Heinz von Foerster's "aesthetical imperative" rings forth: "If you desire to see, learn how to act."[129] Taoists would not disagree, but would complete the idea by proposing the inverse and reverse. While Berry would have us found our action in not-knowing, Lao Tzu would have us find our knowing in not-acting. Such is the notion of *wu wei,* to which we now turn.

## WEI WU WEI / (KNOWING/not-acting)

The term *wu wei* 無 爲, one of the most pivotal in Taoist thought, has commonly been translated in English as "non-action." This is unfortunate, for it can be misinterpreted to mean "not doing anything at all." Richard Wilhelm explains that *wu wei* "is not quietism in our sense, but is the readiness to act the part in the phenomenal world assigned to man by time and his surroundings."[130] In other words, *wu wei* has to do with acting in accord with context.

*Wu* 無 means "no," a negation which originally meant "to vanish."[131] It conveys the sense of emptiness, immanence, and boundlessness, and is thus closely associated with the Tao. Ezra Pound, a poet known more, perhaps, for his uncanny intuitive grasp of Chinese pictograms than for his exhaustive scholarship, and more for luminescent than definitive renderings of Chinese poetry, made the following speculations about the character *wu* 無: "*Not Possessing*. Morrison [editor of a seven-volume Chinese-English dictionary] says: 'Etymology not clear.' It is certainly fire [ˌ ﹀ ﹀] under what looks like a fence [無], but primitive sign does not look like fire but like *bird*. At a wild guess I should say primitive sign looks like 'birdie has flown' (off with the branch). F[enollosa] gives it as 'lost in a forest.'"[132]

*Wei* 爲 means "activity," but it has a double meaning, captured in part by the word "act." *To act* can simply mean "to do," or it can imply a certain artificiality or forced quality. Combining *wu* and *wei* in the phrase *wu wei*, we have the beginnings of a translation: "not acting." Benjamin Hoff achieves an ingenious rendering of *wu wei* by incorporating the pictoral etymology of *wei* in the following manner:

Practically speaking, [*Wu Wei*] means without meddlesome, combative, or egotistical effort. It seems rather significant that the character *Wei* developed from the symbols for a clawing hand and a monkey, since the term *Wu Wei* means not going against the nature of things; no clever tampering; no Monkeying Around.[133]

Hoff's translation—"no monkeying around"—works well for *wu wei,* but it fails to live up to the demands of *wei wu wei* 爲 無 爲 (found, for example, at the beginning of chapter 63 of the *Tao Te Ching*), where the first *wei* carries no negative connotations; "monkeying without monkeying around" does not do justice to the original. John Wu comes closer to conveying the doubleness of *wei* by rendering it as both "do" and "ado" as the occasion requires; *wu wei* becomes "no ado," and the phrase *wei wu wei,* meaning "to act without acting" or "to act without straining," then becomes "doing without ado."[134] In English, our spiral moiré thus reads: DO WITHOUT ADO / (KNOWING / no ado).

There is yet another way of getting the gist of it. John Cage's layering of sound and silence in his "Lecture on Nothing" and Lao Tzu's use of paradox in the first line of the *Tao Te Ching* were earlier described as means of not-saying what needed saying. Different from *not saying,* which, like *nonaction,* suggests only the indifferent absence of something, *not-saying* is an *involved or absorbed absence,* a *necessary gap.* It speaks of the connected absence of the Tao and reflects the complementarity of respect and ignorance mentioned earlier by Berry. Likewise, the "no ado" of *wu wei* can be thought of as not-acting, an action responsive to the demands of the context. As *active emptiness, wu wei* is relationally fitting; it accords with the encompassing (and empty) pattern of the whole.

Two lines in the thirty-seventh chapter of the *Tao Te*

*Ching* concern themselves with the connection between Tao and *wu wei*. But in order to tease out an understanding of Tao's *not-acting* we must ease in again to the con-volutions of Lao Tzu's *not-saying*. Wu translates the passage as:

道 常 無 為

而 無 不 為

Tao never makes any ado,
And yet it does everything.[135]

Missing from the English version are the two negations in the second sentence: *wu* 無 and *pu* 不. The translator presumably decided that they canceled each other out and chose to render the phrase positively: "And yet it does everything." But saying something with a double negative is much different from just stating it in the affirmative.

Hypnotists have long known that to make sense of a simple negation one has to first represent whatever is negated. Because "negation exists only in language and not in experience,"[136] a person cannot experience the suggestions "don't get too comfortable" or "I wouldn't ask you to relax" without imagining the feelings of comfort and relaxation. The hypnotist makes use of this phenomenon to facilitate trance induction.

If a simple negation sends us to its opposite in order to make sense of it, then a double negation sends us in a circle, to both poles of what is being said and not said. Like the reciprocal definition of yin and yang, a double negation involves an assertion and its counter in a mutual proposing that never resolves to one side of the distinction. Lao Tzu's use of negation, like his use of paradox, is a strategy of con-volution for talking in the gaps, for not-talking about the recursiveness of Tao. Something of the spirit in the Chinese can be retained by modifying Wu's second line in the following way:

> Tao never makes any ado,
> But is never not doing.

However, the original's crisp flow, parallel structure, and not-saying can be more fully appreciated if both lines are re-translated as:

Tao forever not-acts
But never not acts

As was mentioned earlier, the not-acting of *wu wei* is a means of participatory knowing. This stands in stark contrast to the traditional scientific orientation wherein the knower stands apart and researches by means of duress. Morris Berman characterizes this legacy of the Scientific Revolution: "Knowledge of nature comes about under artificial conditions. Vex nature, disturb it, alter it, anything—but do not leave it alone. Then, and only then, will you know it."[137] For a Taoist, knowledge is a question of fit—it comes about not by manipulating nature, but by attuning 正 to it, by adapting 柔 to its course. The famous Taoist philosopher Chuang Tzu (circa 300 B.C.E.) aptly illustrates the point in a fictional story about Confucius and a man who has mastered the art of *wu wei*:

> Confucius was seeing the sights at Lü-liang, where the water
> falls from a height of thirty fathoms and races and boils along

for forty li, so swift that no fish or other water creature can swim in it. He saw a man dive into the water and, supposing that the man was in some kind of trouble and intended to end his life, he ordered his disciples to line up on the bank and pull the man out. But after the man had gone a couple of hundred paces, he came out of the water and began strolling along the base of the embankment, his hair streaming down, singing a song. Confucius ran after him and said, "At first I thought you were a ghost, but now I see you're a man. May I ask if you have some special way of staying afloat in the water?"

"I have no way. I began with what I was used to, grew up with my nature, and let things come to completion with fate. I go under with the swirls and come out with the eddies, following along the way the water goes and never thinking about myself. That's how I can stay afloat." [138]

Wu wei is knowing via immersement. Like the action of an artist who soaks into his or her work, it is undertaken for its own sake, rather than for some removed purpose. Gary Snyder relates the story of one of Basho's disciples,

who took down something Basho once said to a group of students. He said, "To learn about the pine, go to the pine. To learn about the bamboo, go to the bamboo. But this learn is not just what you think learn is. You only learn by becoming totally absorbed in that which you wish to learn. There are many people who think that they have learned something and willfully construct a poem which is artifice and does not flow from their delicate entrance into the life of another object." [139]

This full involvement is not, however, an expression of connection alone. In contrast to the "ex-orbitance" of purposeful attainment (which hangs onto only one side of a distinction), the emptiness of wei wu wei strikes a fundamental balance between the connection of knowing and the separation of not-acting—WEI WU WEI / (IMMERSED KNOWING / not-acting)—as this passage from the *I Ching* conveys:

> "ex-orbitant" speaks of:
> knowing when to step forward but not backward
> accepting life but not death
> knowing when to grasp but not to let go
> only sages know when to step forward and backward
> how to accept life and death
> do not slip from attunement
> only sages[140]

In recursively joining both sides of the connection/separation distinction, both sides of life and death, *wu wei* is not-one-not-two action, a *knowing (no-ing) act of completion* and a *complete act of knowing (no-ing)*.

The *circularity* of completion is of especial importance in Taoist thought and warrants a section devoted to its elucidation. The discussion will begin with an investigation of the root meanings of four Chinese characters that appear at the beginning and throughout the *I Ching*. The final, fourth, word of the series is particularly puzzling—its meaning in this context has stumped commentators of the book for centuries. The interpretation developed here hinges on a piece of abductive reasoning: a critical clue is sought, and found, in the work of Bateson.[141] The resulting understanding provides the necessary groundwork for completing the chapter—with a discussion of the mind of knowing, the Mind of Nature, and the nature of wisdom.

## COMPLETION / (LIFE/death)

Within the circles of our lives
we dance the circles of the years,

the circles of the seasons
within the circles of the years,
the cycles of the moon
within the circles of the seasons,
the circles of our reasons
within the cycles of the moon.

—*Wendell Berry*


If our explanations or our understanding of the universe is in some sense to match that universe, or model it, and if the universe is recursive, then our explanations and our logics must also be fundamentally recursive.

—*Gregory Bateson*


There are four words in the *I Ching*—*yüan, heng, li,* and *chen*—that together compose what Iulian Shchutskii calls a "mantic formulae."[142] They occur frequently in different combinations throughout the book, but first appear at the very beginning, immediately following the title of the first chapter, "*Ch'ien.*"

乾　Ch'ien

元　yüan

亨　heng

利　li

貞　chen

Shchutskii believes that these mantic terms belong to the oldest strata of the book, "remnants of a much earlier system of divination,"[143] but that their original meanings have been lost. Because of the ambiguous nature of ancient Chinese, there is no way of determining exactly how the phrase should be punctuated, and thus interpreted. It can be read as a single sentence: *Ch'ien yüan heng li chen*. Or, alternatively, it can be understood as a kind of list—*Ch'ien: yüan, heng, li, chen*—where the latter four words, each relatively independent, explicate the meaning of the first.

Richard Wilhelm, choosing the first alternative, translates the phrase as:

> THE CREATIVE works sublime success,
> Furthering through perseverance.[144]

Shchutskii finds it "difficult to agree with such an interpretation since a construction so highly developed in grammatical relations would hardly be possible in such an archaic text."[145] It also produces a sentence so abstract that it is virtually meaningless. The alternative—treating the terms as different dimensions or aspects of *Ch'ien*—is more in keeping with the paratactic structure of ancient Chinese, and it correctly confers equal importance on all four words.[146] By looking closely at the etymologies of *Ch'ien* and the other four characters, it is possible to recover something of their original meanings and to suggest an interpretation of the phrase as a whole.

Wilhelm's translation of *Ch'ien* 乾 as "The Creative" is accurate, but incomplete. The archaic form of the character 乾 depicts the sun 日 (heat, light, creativity) between the roots 乡 and branches 屮 of a plant (the beginning and end of growth). The symbol on the right 乙 is an abbreviated form of *ch'i* 氣, or "life-breath." The translation "Enflaming[147] Inspiration" suggests the combination of the elemental light of the sun and the breath-like nature of *ch'i* (*inspiration* is from the Latin *in* and *spirare*—"to breathe in"); it speaks of the complete life process, from beginning (roots) to end (branches).

The top stroke — of *yüan* 元 means "one" or "first" and

thus suggests the notion of inception or beginning. The lower portion of the character 兀 probably depicts the foundation from which the "originating" begins. The second word of the four, *heng* 亨, speaks of unobstructed process and development: a smooth flow 了 issues from an opening 口: it "flows freely." *Li* 利 is a picture of the fruit ノ of mature crops 禾 being harvested with a cutting implement 刂. It thus refers to a ripeness of a situation, a time when one's effort "bears fruit."

*Chen* 貞, the last of the four mantic terms, is very curious: It literally means to divine 卜 with a tortoise shell 貝, a practice dating to the Shang dynasty (1766–1122 B.C.E.). Having been asked a question of import, a diviner would heat a tortoise shell over a fire until it cracked and then interpret the resultant random scattering of lines. However, within the context of "Enflaming Inspiration" and the other three characters, it is clear that *chen* is not being used in its literal sense (i.e., as "to divine"):

Enflaming Inspiration
  originates
  flows freely
  bears fruit
  *chen*

The sequence "originates/ flows freely/ bears fruit" appears to describe the phases of a life process, from the beginning, through development, and on to maturation. What then is the fourth phase of "Enflaming Inspiration," and how does divination fit into this cycle? Looking beyond the perimeters of Taoism, we find an important hint in Bateson:

Ross Ashby long ago pointed out that no system (neither computer nor organism) can produce anything *new* unless the system contains some source of the random. In the computer, this will be a random-number generator which will ensure that the "seeking," trial-and-error moves of the machine will ultimately cover all the possibilities of the set to be explored.

In other words, all innovative, *creative* systems are . . . *divergent.*[148]

The essential element in divination is its *unpredictability,* its incorporation of the *random* in the formulation of answers. The diviner has no control over the way in which the tortoise shell will crack. And it is to this notion of *divergence* that *chen,* in this context, most probably refers. In order for the creative cycle of Enflaming Inspiration to return to an *original* beginning, there must be a period of dis-integration, a time following maturation where seeds scatter and organic matter breaks down and returns to the soil. As Bateson puts it, "The ongoing processes of change *feed on the random.*"[149] And again:

> For the creation of new order, the workings of the random, the plethora of uncommitted alternatives (entropy) is necessary. It is out of the random that organisms collect new mutations, and it is there that stochastic learning gathers its solutions. Evolution leads to climax: ecological saturation of all the possibilities of differentiation. Learning leads to the overpacked mind. By return to the unlearned and mass-produced egg, the ongoing species again and again clears its memory banks to be ready for the new.[150]

The sequence is now complete:

元 originates

亨 flows freely

利 bears fruit

貞 diversifies

The scattering denoted by "diversifies" is the unravelling of pattern, the separation of death that brings life to completion and makes it possible for it to begin again. In Chuang Tzu's words:

> Life is the companion of death, death is the beginning of life. Who understands their workings? Man's life is a coming-together of breath. If it comes together, there is life; if it scatters, there is death. And if life and death are companions to each other, then what is there for us to be anxious about?[151]

When the cyclic process of renewal elaborated by the four terms *yüan, heng, li,* and *chen* is laconically expressed as the imbricated moiré COMPLETION / (LIFE/death), a correspondence can be marked between this pattern of living process and the pattern of mind delineated in the complementarity COMPLETION / (CONNECTION/separation). There is resonance between the organization of knowing and the organization of the living—each is metaphoric of the other. Just as the wholeness of knowing is a process of completing the connections and separations of drawn distinctions, so the wholeness of an ecosystem is a process of completing the connections and separations of life and death. The mind of knowing must sever in order to connect; the Mind of Nature must sever in order to live: Nature knows itself (i.e., recursively sets the limits of its organization, defines the thresholds of its structure) by drawing distinctions with the knife of death.[152] And just as the mind of knowing is threatened if unconnected separations hold sway, so too, as Bateson articulates below, the survival of the Mind of Nature rests entirely on its continued success at *encompassing* death.

> Nature avoids (temporarily) what looks like irreversible change by accepting ephemeral change. "The bamboo bends before the wind," in Japanese metaphor; and death itself is avoided

by a quick change from individual subject to class. Nature, to personify the system, allows old man Death (also personified) to have his individual victims while she substitutes that more abstract entity, the class of taxon, to kill which Death must work faster than the reproductive systems of the creatures. Finally, if Death should have his victory over the species, Nature will say, "Just what I needed for my ecosystem." [153]

Left to its own devices, an ecosystem evolves in the direction of complexity, weaving life and death in a regenerative balance known as *climax*. Gary Snyder describes it this way:

This condition, called "climax," is an optimum condition of diversity—optimum stability. When a system reaches climax, it levels out for centuries or millennia. By virtue of its diversity it has the capacity to absorb all sorts of impacts. Insects, fungi, weather conditions come and go; it's the opposite of monoculture. . . . Another aspect of a climax situation is that almost half of the energy that flows in the system does not come from annual growth, it comes from the recycling of dead growth. . . . This is also what is called "maturity." By some oddity in the language it's also what we call a virgin forest, although it's actually very experienced, wise, and mature. [154]

The Mind of Nature is wise and healthy when its cycles are complete, when it enfolds death as a part of the ongoing renewal and complexity of its wholeness. There are no monotone or transitive "values" in biology, says Bateson, nothing of which there can always be more. Death is the calibration that establishes the thresholds and thus regulates the living balance of the whole:

Desired substances, things, patterns, or sequences of experience that are in some sense "good" for the organism—items of diet, conditions of life, temperature, entertainment, sex, and so forth—are never such that more of the something is always better than less of the something. Rather, for all objects and experiences, there is a quantity that has optimum value. Above that quantity, the variable becomes toxic. To fall below that value is to be deprived.[155]

There can even be too much "life." Cancer cells don't know when to die and thus they undermine the balance of the system of which they are a part. In trespassing beyond the thresholds of the organism, they trigger its death.

The mind of knowing, in turn, is wise—that is, in Bateson's terms, it has "a sense or recognition of the fact of circuity"[156]—and healthy (i.e., whole) when dichotomous distinctions are joined and actions are complete:

Half then whole
Bent then straight
Hollow then full
Worn then new
Little then gains
Plenty then perplexed[157]

Commenting on the last two lines of this passage from the *Tao Te Ching*, Wang Pi (226–249 C.E.) highlights the problem of not attending to cyclic balance:

The Tao of *Tzu-jan* [i.e., being true to one's nature] is like a tree. The more it grows (to have plenty), the more distant it is from the roots; the less it grows (to have little), the less distant it is from the roots. If one always increases, then one becomes removed from the true essence.[158]

*Wu wei* is the not-acting of this circuitous knowing. The wisdom is reflected in knowing *how* to complete and knowing *when* the completion has been reached. Wendell Berry tells the story of a barber he once knew who refused to give a discount to a bald client, explaining that his artistry consisted, not in the cutting off, but in the knowing when to stop. He spoke, I think, as a true artist and a true human. The lack of such knowledge is extremely dangerous in and to an individual. But ignorance of when to stop is a modern epidemic; it is the basis of "industrial progress" and "economic growth."[159]

Despite its cyclic timing—knowing when to stop and when to begin—the complete knowing of *wu wei*, however participatory, is necessarily a not-knowing of completion. This ensures a certain humility and respect in encountering the wholes of which one is a part. Lao Tzu warns:

> The world is a sacred vessel, which must not be tampered
> with or grabbed after.
> To tamper with it is to spoil it, and to grasp it is to lose it.[160]

The ideas set forth in this chapter, unpacked from the spiral complementarity COMPLETION / (CONNECTION/separation), have made many connections and left much not-said. The moirés—and the moirés of moirés—that have emerged will, in the next chapter, be used as guides for contextually patterning the shortcut intentionality of conscious mind and the problems that swirl in its wake.

# 3 CONTRACTION \ [SEPARATION \ connection]

Take heed of hating me,
Or too much triumph in the victory;
Not that I shall be mine own officer,
And hate with hate again retaliate;
But thou wilt lose the style of conqueror,
If I thy conquest, perish by thy hate.
Then, lest my being nothing lessen thee,
If thou hate me, take heed of hating me.

—*John Donne*

Unaided consciousness must always tend toward hate; not only because it is good common sense to exterminate the other fellow, but for the more profound reason that, seeing only arcs of circuits, the individual is continually surprised and necessarily angered when his hardheaded policies return to plague the inventor.

—*Gregory Bateson*

Any organism that destroys what it takes to be its other, not recognizing itself in that other, lays a firm foundation for self-destruction.

—*Edward E. Sampson*

Desire is the presence of an *absence*.

—*Alexandre Kojeve*

A person who thinks of a boomerang as just a slab wood will be puzzled when attempts to throw it away continually fail. Similarly, a person who thinks of hate as pure *repulsion* (from the Latin *re-*, "back," and *pellere*, "to drive") will be repeatedly perplexed at how *compelling* (from the Latin *com-*, "together," and *pellere*, "to drive") the object of hate becomes.

The mirror reflection of hate is desire. Whereas the separation of hate effects a connection, the connection of desire is an effect of separation: Once the object of desire is gained the desire of the object is lost.

Common to both hate and desire is the *inversion of wholeness* indicated in the title of this chapter. In contradistinction to the imbricated shape of *health* formalized in the whole/part matrix COMPLETION / (CONNECTION/separation), the model CONTRACTION \ [SEPARATION\connection] defines the inverted, fractionated shape of *defection* (from the Latin *defect-us*, "defect," "want"). The *Oxford English Dictionary* defines *defection* as "the action or fact of . . . falling short."[1] A *defect* has to do with "the fact of being wanting or falling short; lack or absence of something essential to completeness."[2] The pattern of contraction—

CONTRACTION \ [SEPARATION\connection]

—is, in this sense, a *defective* version of

COMPLETION / (CONNECTION/separation)

Contraction falls short of completion. The word *contraction* (from the Latin *con-*, "together" + *trahere*, "to pull, draw") means to draw together, to narrow, limit, or shorten. As when a muscle contracts, such shortening is accompanied by an attendant tightness. Similarly, in the world of grammar, *contraction* refers to a word that has been shortened by the omission of medial letters or sounds. As the contrary of completion, contraction is not simply noncompletion or incompletion; it is used here to connote a tightened, shortened *connection*, a constriction that, in falling short of health, *precludes* completion. As we shall see below, contraction is a short-circuited parody of the long-circuited wholeness of completion.

The order and capitalization of items in COMPLETION / (CONNECTION/separation) denotes the spiral of their whole/part layering. CONNECTION contextualizes separation, and COMPLETION, which connects CONNECTION and separation, contextualizes them both. In the wound-up dichotomy CONTRACTION \ [SEPARATION\connection], *the contextual stacking of connection and separation is inverted*, with the latter now embedding the former. This difference is highlighted by the reversal of the direction of the slashes and the placement of SEPARATION\connection in square brackets.

With completion, connections relax and resolve to dissolution. Separation (the scattering of patterns) follows (and thus precedes) connection in continual recursive process:

元   originates

亨   flows freely

利   bears fruit

貞   diversifies

But contraction is always a "shortcoming," and thus such resolution is never reached—the denial of the *simultaneity* of connection and separation (i.e., treating distinctions only as severance) denies their *succession* and thus precludes their success. This is the pattern of paradox that Bateson terms the *double bind*.[3] The schismatic bond that binds is one that cannot complete—within contraction, separation and connection continually undermine each other: The moment they succeed they fail. *Hate prevents the separation it desires and desire invents the separation it hates.*

Confronted with the short-circuits of symptoms such as hate and desire, family therapists are accustomed to reflecting on their underlying purpose. As interesting as this line of reasoning can be, an even more intriguing proposition emerges if we reverse the logic of the formulation: rather than explore the purpose of symptoms, this chapter considers problems as symptoms of purpose. Intricately lacing the unconnected separations of all contractions is the peculiar ig-norance of conscious knowing.

# SHORT-CIRCUIT \
## [CONSCIOUS KNOWING \
purpose]

不 知 Knowing ignorance: tiptop
知 不 Ignorant knowing: defective
知 知 —*Lao Tzu*
病 上 La peste de l'homme, c'est l'opinion de savoir.
(Mankind's plague is the conceit of knowing.)
—*Michel de Montaigne*

It may well be that consciousness contains systematic distortions of view which, when implemented by modern technology, become destructive of the balances between man, his society, and his ecosystem.
—*Gregory Bateson*

Properly embedded in the total weave of Mind, consciousness functions much as its position in this whole/part pattern of mental process would suggest:

MIND / (UNCONSCIOUS/conscious)

Consciousness, which takes the place of "separation" in the matrix COMPLETION / (CONNECTION/separation), knows by dissecting and analyzing, by *separating*.

Included within and connected to relational knowing (i.e., to "unconscious" or "primary" processes such as dreams, art, and "feelings"),[4] such divisiveness adaptively fits and contributes to the completion of Mind. Indeed, Roy Rappaport believes that purposefulness (which he takes to be a concomitant of consciousness) has undoubtedly contributed substantially to humankind's survival during our three million years' residency on the planet.[5] However, it is perhaps to be expected that conscious knowing—predicated as it is on separation—should tend to self-reflexively split itself off from the balance of Mind, from the body and its social and biological contexts. Bateson discusses how unmediated consciousness necessarily distorts the interactive circularity of mental process. When the sense of participatory knowing is deposed, the non-sense of divisive knowing is imposed.

> If the total mind and the outer world do not, in general, have this lineal structure, then by forcing this structure upon them, we become blind to the cybernetic circularities of the self and the external world. Our conscious sampling of data will not disclose whole circuits but only arcs of circuits, cut off from their matrix by our selective attention.[6]

Unfortunately, any goal-directed (purposeful) action taken within such a context of fissured knowing will necessarily fall short of wisdom. Purpose is rather like a race horse with blinders: chiefly concerned with getting from point A to point B in the most direct way and in the shortest possible time, it suffers the effects of tunnel-vision. Consciousness, says Bateson,

> is organized in terms of purpose. It is a short-cut device to enable you to get quickly at what you want; not to act with maximum wisdom in order to live, but to follow the shortest logical or causal path to get what you next want. . . .
>
> Purposive consciousness pulls out, from the total mind, sequences which do not have the loop structure which is characteristic of the whole systemic structure. If you follow the "common-sense" dictates of consciousness you become, effectively, greedy and unwise.[7]

With single-focused attention riveted on end goals, consciousness grasps for only one side of distinctions, as opposed to clinging to both sides:[8] A desired "good" is isolated and pursued as if it were an independent entity, as if there were no limit to it, no threshold beyond which it stops being good, and no recognition that there is *always* another side to the coin. Such lopsided logic renders consciousness ig-norant of the simple wisdom of Lao Tzu:

物 或 損 之 而 益
或 益 之 而 損

things may gain by losing
     may lose by gaining[9]

Gary Snyder tells a story of when he was a student of Zen in Japan:

> During the first year or two that I was at Daitoku-ji Sodo . . . I noticed a number of times little improvements that could be made. Ultimately I ventured to suggest to the head monks some labor- and time-saving techniques. They were tolerant of

me for a while. Finally, one day one of them took me aside and said, "We don't want to do things any better or any faster, because that's not the point—the point is that you live the whole life. If we speed up the work in the garden, you'll just have to spend that much more time sitting in the zendo [meditation hall], and your legs will hurt more." It's all one meditation. The importance is in the right balance, and not how to save time in one place or another.[10]

Lao Tzu's recursive logic and the monk's wisdom are echoed in Bateson's descriptions of biological systems as balanced, *multipurposed* circuits.

There is no single variable in the redwood forest of which we can say that the whole system is oriented to maximizing that variable and all other variables are subsidiary to it; and, indeed, the redwood forest works toward optima, not maxima. Its needs are satiable, and too much of anything is toxic.[11]

The poet e. e. cummings weaves it this way:

whatever's merely wilful,
and not miraculous
(be never it so skilful)
must wither fail and cease
—but better than to grow
beauty knows no[12]

The "no" beauty knows is *threshold*, a boundary within a whole, a separation contextualized by the connection of "yes." By saying no to the skillful purpose of the particular, the whole says yes to the miraculous, to the aesthetic balance of the relational pattern which connects:

BEAUTY / (YES/no)

But like Faust, consciousness becomes narcissistically intoxicated by the "beauty" of its own short-term successes.

Losing sight of "no," of what it cannot know, consciousness does not keep its place in Mind in mind. If left uncalibrated, its lineality of focus and action will, in the service of expediency, clear-cut a swath through the delicate complexity of living relationships as it invades and colonizes domains of Mind beyond its ken.

"If a man entertain false opinions regarding his own nature," Bateson cautions, "he will be led thereby to courses of action which will be in some profound sense immoral or ugly." [13] Ugliness knows the "no" of ig-norance and the "yes" of unrestricted growth:

UGLINESS \ [NO\yes]

Such "per-version" of beauty is a short-circuited contraction reflecting the severance (separation) of consciousness from the larger Mind and the attachment (connection) of purpose to singular goals:

SHORT-CIRCUIT \ [CONSCIOUS KNOWING \ purpose]

Bateson provides illustration:

> We will imagine a steady state process going along on the hillside of Ponderosa pines, and the pines are balancing out with the deer and the cactuses and all the rest of the living things there. What are they called? "Sentient beings." Now in come you and I, and of the various variables on that hillside, we decide to maximize one. . . .
>
> Now what happened? What happened was that the human beings identified *a* variable, looked at the immediate predecessors of that variable in the general train, and started with what sophistication they could to maximize these in order to maximize the one they wanted. But they have totally ignored three quarters of the whole circle, you see. . . . [which means they] are going to wreck the balances. [14]

Not knowing its ignorance, consciousness becomes ignorant knowing, and this, as Lao Tzu correctly diagnoses in the quotation at the beginning of this section, is defective.[15] Bateson offers a diagnosis:

> Mere purposive rationality unaided by such phenomena as art, religion, dream, and the like, is necessarily pathogenic and destructive of life; and . . . its virulence springs specifically from the circumstance that life depends upon interlocking *circuits* of contingency, while consciousness can see only such short arcs of such circuits as human purpose may direct.[16]

Even when the discord between Mind and unmediated consciousness is recognized, it is very difficult to do anything that does not simply make matters worse. Solutions that do not escape the dualistic assumptions of conscious knowing will themselves become symptomatic expressions of purpose, hopelessly entangled in the problems they are helplessly trying to eradicate.[17] In fact, it is precisely this attempt to *eradicate problems* that secures the failure of dichotomous solutions and guarantees an exacerbation of the original situation. Solution and problem are mutually defined; it is impossible for one side of a distinction to destroy the other side—*any* oppositional response only highlights the relationship, thus intensifying the problem and reiterating its intractability:

SHORT-CIRCUIT \
    [DISJUNCTIVE SOLUTION\conjunctive problem]

This transform of the analytic matrix CONTRACTION \ [SEPARATION\connection], where repelling (disjunctive) solutions circle endlessly with compelling (conjunctive) problems, defines a pattern commonly identified as *addiction*.

# ADDICTION \
## [DISJUNCTIVE SOLUTION \
## conjunctive problem]

What then is a shortcut? What is wrong with the proposed shortcuts in evolution and in the resolution of guilt? What is wrong, in principle, with shortcuts?

*—Gregory Bateson*

Mastery as the remedy becomes the poison.

*—Edward Sampson*

Vicious circles are what biology lives on, but you've got to have a world in which that is all the time being held in control.

*—Gregory Bateson*

People who respond to the close presence of bees by flailing their arms and trying to slap them away are not only usually unsuccessful in ridding themselves of the source of their fear, but their actions attract the bees, thus heightening their danger of being stung. All disjunctive solutions—where one tries to quickly destroy or banish or defeat a problem—have something of this flailing-at-bees quality about them, and all conjunctive problems are rather bee-like in character: that is, such problems hover around those who attempt to repel them, and their sting can be painful and dangerous.

The dichotomous definition of a problem as something in need of a quick and complete solution establishes the very context of separation that precludes the possibility of completion. It is in this way that the tight, addictive circles of problem and solution are continually respun:

SHORT-CIRCUIT ADDICTION \
    [DISJUNCTIVE SOLUTION \ conjunctive problem]

As will be discussed in the next chapter, completion is only possible within a context of connection, where the relaxed immersement of long-circuit adaptation replaces the frantic drowning of short-circuit addiction:

LONG-CIRCUIT ADAPTATION / (IMMERSEMENT/dispersement)

The short-circuit of addiction is an adaptation of sorts, but one that does not complete. It is, by definition, a vicious circle. In adapting to some item of experience—be it a relationship with a person, object, chemical, behavior, attitude, or belief—addiction provides short-term benefits; but when continued beyond a certain threshold (of time or quantity) it is destructive of more inclusive levels of systemic organization (e.g., physiological, psychological, social, and ecological relationships):

ADDICTION \
    [FISSION OF SYSTEMIC RELATIONSHIPS \
      fusion to particular item of experience]

According to Bateson, adaptation and addiction "are *very* closely related phenomena."[18] For example, drugs such as alcohol, nicotine, cocaine, and tranquilizers can alter the metabolism of a person in a way that is experienced as "pleasurable." If usage continues over time, the metabolism may adapt in such a way that the *absence* of the drug is experienced as "painful." The continuation (or increase) of the drug level has immediate adapative advantages (avoidance of pain, experience of relief or pleasure) but extended addictive drawbacks: In addition to destroying organs in the body system, the addiction can also undermine relationships with family members, co-workers, friends, and so on, who organize their behavior around the person's intake of the drug. In striving to deal effectively (purposefully) with the situation, other people get inducted into the cycle of addiction—they too are caught in the creation and maintenance of the vicious cycle.

It should not be surprising that addiction commonly entails an *escalating* process, given that it is grounded in the transitive values of purpose. Addiction is a solution that is ignorant of thresholds: Like money, more is always thought to be better than less. For instance, the adaptive development of nuclear weaponry that so expediently brought World War II to an end has become a systemic addiction infecting America's economy, military strategy, and foreign policy. Gregory Bateson and Mary Catherine Bateson inscribe the spiral: "The armaments boys are addicted to feeling not just strong but stronger—stronger than yesterday and stronger than the Russians. The arms race both leaves us vulnerable to war and tends to escalate." [19]

If a system positions itself toward maximizing or minimizing one variable in its repertoire, the balance maintained by interactive complexity will be lost. Our consumer economy, what Wendell Berry refers to below as a "little economy," is a case in point. Addicted to increasing "wealth," individuals and businesses adapt in order to grow richer, and in so doing trivialize the natural environment (a more encompassing system than human society) from which the wealth is ultimately drawn.

> An explosive economy . . . is not only an economy that is dependent upon explosions but also one that sets no limits on itself. Any little economy that sees itself as unlimited is obviously self-blinded. It does not see its real relation of dependence and obligation to the Great Economy; in fact, it does not see that there *is* a Great Economy. Instead it calls the Great

Economy "raw material" or "natural resources" or "nature" and proceeds with the business of putting it "under control." [20]

In order to maximize the earnings of our little economy, we minimize controls on the waste we return to the Great Economy, producing such symptoms as acid rain and acid lakes. In applying solutions to these perceived problems, we, like all addicts, fail to question our premises, proceeding instead to *apply a purposive solution at the level at which we recognize the problem.* If there is too much acid in the lakes, we add lime to adjust the pH balance. The more effective this practice is in restoring a *semblance* of balance at the level of the particular, the more it will contribute to an inclusive addictive imbalance.

Shortcuts create short-circuits when they cross-cut contextual layers, when they breach or confuse what Bateson refers to as levels of logical type:

> In a large variety of cases, perhaps in all cases in which the shortcut generates trouble—the root of the matter is an error in logical typing. Somewhere in the sequence of actions and ideas, we can expect to find a class treated as though it were one of its members; or a member treated as though it were identical with the class; a uniqueness treated as a generality or a generality treated as a uniqueness. It is legitimate (and usual) to think of a process or change as an ordered class of states, but a mistake to think of any one of these states as if it were the class of which it is only a member. [21]

As contractions of the long-circuited solutions of cybernetic Mind, short-circuits are mistyped as completions and thus are condemned to repeat themselves over and over again. They are enacted as if they were a *class of solution* (i.e., a long-term adaptation) when in fact they are just *ad hoc* measures that leave uncorrected the deeper causes of the trouble and, worse, usually permit those causes to grow stronger and become compounded. In medicine, to relieve the symptoms without curing the disease is wise and sufficient *if and only if* either the disease is surely terminal *or* will cure itself.[22]

In their failure to account for inclusive patterns of relationship, *ad hoc* responses remain disjunctively separate, isolated and apart from the contexts of which they are a part.

Inebriation can be understood as an alcoholic's *ad hoc* adaptation—a short-term, and therefore dichotomous, solution applied at the same level of organization as problems in his or her sobriety. Bateson points out that if a drinker's

style of sobriety drives him to drink, then that style must contain error or pathology; and intoxication must provide some—at least subjective—correction of this error. In other words, compared with his sobriety, which is in some way "wrong," his intoxication must be in some way "right."[23]

Drinking can be considered purposeful to the extent that it is an expedient and single-leveled solution. And the more immediately "right" it is, and the more often the solution is invoked, the greater the later and more enveloping "wrong" it creates. The premises that give rise to addictive solutions are not undermined by failure; the person is simply challenged to do a better job of enacting them the next time around. As Bateson explains, "The premises of 'purpose' are simply not of the same logical type as the material facts of life, and therefore cannot easily be contradicted by them."[24]

Problem and attempted solution thus circle and become one, continually evoking the contractions of conscious knowing: that is, that there can be connection without separation and separation without connection, good without bad, unlimited growth without unlimited consequences, shortcuts without short-circuits, and so on. Further, and more important, the contextual bungling of addictive solutions reveals a fundamental mistyping of the relationship between whole and part. In order to trace this error, we must first distinguish the nature of complementary and symmetrical relationships.[25]

Complementary relationships are characterized by *co-operative difference,* where the behaviors of A and B mutually fit each other by virtue of their distinctiveness (e.g., dominance-submission, exhibitionism-spectatorship, nurturance-dependency, and so on). Symmetry, on the other hand, is a pattern of *competitive sameness*—opposition between participants is a kind of mirror reflection, such that the more A acts in a particular way, the more B symmetrically responds in kind (e.g., the fighting of boxers or the sprinting of racers). Note how the difference necessary for complementarity—

COMPLEMENTARITY / (COOPERATION/difference)

—is a cooperative connection that echoes COMPLETION / (CONNECTION/separation), whereas the sameness of symmetry is a function of an oppositional separation that mirrors CONTRACTION \ [SEPARATION\connection]:

SYMMETRY \ [OPPOSITION\sameness]

The mirrored opposition of symmetrical relationships ensures that both A and B will confront each other at the same logical level (as in the hegelian dialectic described in the last chapter). Similarly, the competition between opponents in a tennis match, as embodied in the rules for serving and hitting, scoring, winning, and so on, is between two "equal" participants. The game is *not* played between an individual and the tennis club to which he or she belongs; that is, it is not between a member and a class, not between a part and a whole, but between two members within the same context— in this case, two tennis players.

However, the situation is more complex with complementarity. While it is possible for the complementary differences between A and B to be of the same contextual order (as in the relationship between a teacher and a student, each of whom are members of a context called a school), it is also true that *any part of either a complementary or symmetrical relationship is always complementary to the relationship as a whole, to the context.* Thus the teacher and student are each complementary to the learning context they together define, just as the symmetrical tennis players are each complementary to the game they together play:

WHOLE/PART COMPLEMENTARITY /

((PART/PART COMPLEMENTARITY) / (part/part symmetry))

Another way of giving shape to this is to talk in terms of survival. For a relationship to endure, whether it be complementary or symmetrical, the participants must necessarily cooperate in its maintenance. Even competitive opposition is always nested within cooperation:

COOPERATION / (COMPLEMENTARITY/symmetry)

This is where conscious purpose makes its fatal error. Whereas competition is an either/or relationship organized to reap short-term gain, the both/and structure of cooperation is necessary if long-term survival is to obtain. Competition is not a problem if it is cooperatively contextualized (as in a friendly tennis match), but serious problems arise when the relationship between whole and part is mistyped as competitive. A member of a class simply cannot be symmetrically equal to the class of which it is a part; and if it acts as if it *is* possible, addictive disaster cannot help but ensue: "By living in opposition to nature," Berry argues, "we can *cause* natural calamities of which we would otherwise be free."[26] The analytic dichotomy of this is a pattern of addictive defection:

COMPETITION \ [SYMMETRY\complementarity]

Anthony Wilden clarifies that the unit of survival "is not *either* this organism (species, etc.) *or* that, nor *either* organism *or* environment, nor *either* this side of the line *or* that. *It is both-and.*"[27] It is not a matter of the survival of the fittest, but rather the *survival of the fit*. Berry continues: "Competitiveness cannot be the ruling principle, for the Great Economy is not a 'side' that we can join nor are there such 'sides' within it."[28] Wilden again:

> The dominant ideology has long been one which places mankind in a relationship of opposition to nature. Such a relationship of opposition is pathological, not just because it is exploitative (which does after all provide a simple ethical justification for calling it pathological), but rather because it substitutes short-range survival value (competition) for long-range survival value (cooperation).[29]

Out of ig-norance of connective long-term patterns of cooperative interaction, conscious purpose will always be tempted to maximize short-term gain for what it mistakes to be an isolated, independent component of a larger system. Violence and exploitation are "quick-fixes" that are "successful" in furthering the immediate goals of one side of a relationship, but only at the expense of the relationship as whole. Edward Sampson describes how winning can lose:

> In the single-minded pursuit of mastery, the pursuer becomes the pursued, trapped by the very lures and snares established to catch and dominate the presumed "enemy." The very tools and institutions established in the first place to achieve mastery become the source of the new problems that humanity confronts. . . . What is called for, therefore, is a different relationship between humanity and nature, one that partakes less of mastery and more of participation and receptivity.[30]

The alcoholic enacts participation and receptivity, but at the wrong contextual level. The symmetry (competitive separation) of conscious purpose is balanced by complementarity (cooperative connection), but the corrective is introduced as intoxication; as a "quick-fix," inebriation contributes to, and leaves unchallenged, the more encompassing competitive relationship between drinker and bottle.[31] The alcoholic is caught in the double bind of an analytic dichotomy—in order to *continue to win* the battle against the bottle, the drinker must repeatedly engage it in competition:

COMPETITION \

    [SYMMETRICAL BATTLE WITH BOTTLE \

      complementarity of intoxication]

The alcoholic is blind to the fact that this ongoing opposition is a contracted form of cooperation, that the symmetrical interaction with the bottle defines a complementarity between the drinker and the drinking relationship as a whole. As in all contractions, the competitive relationship between drinker and bottle can never complete; success of a particular battle ensures the continuation of the war. When a relationship is predicated on competition, winning (attempting to separate from the bottle by beating it) and losing (connecting to the bottle by continuing to drink) are each ways of maintaining the competition, of maintaining the relationship. Winning is not a way out of the relationship but a way back in.

COMPETITION \ [WINNING \ losing]

The reasons for this go back to the heart of knowing, to the way in which distinctions structure our experience. As George Kelly says, "Much of our language, as well as our everyday thinking, implies contrast which it does not explicitly state." [32] We are continually tripped up by the connections of our separations. The alcoholic's competitive opposition to the bottle is an attempt to get rid of his or her drinking problem by forcefully separating from it. But it is impossible to get to a place where drinking isn't an issue by taking issue with it. Desired separation forges a connection: *Not-drinking* only makes sense in relation to *drinking*. Bateson emphasizes the importance of such mutuality in the world of information (which is organized in terms of difference, or distinctions) by describing the functioning of the nervous system:

> From a systems-theoretic point of view, it is a misleading metaphor to say that what travels in an axon is an "impulse." It would be more correct to say that what travels is a difference, or a transform of a difference. The metaphor of "impulse" suggests a hard-science line of thought which will ramify only too easily into nonsense . . . and those who talk this kind of nonsense will disregard the information content of *quiescence*. The quiescence of an axon *differs* as much from activity as its activity does from quiescence. Therefore quiescence and activity have equal informational relevance. The message of activity can only be accepted as valid if the message of quiescence can also be trusted. . . .
>
> Always the fact that information is a transform of difference should be remembered, and we might better call the one message "activity—not quiescence" and the other "quiescence—not activity."
>
> Similar considerations apply to the repentant alcoholic. He cannot simply elect "sobriety." At best he could only elect "sobriety—not drunkenness," and his universe remains polarized, carrying always both alternatives. [33]

This doubleness of knowing renders change singularly difficult. The desire for absence exacts presence. This is the paradox of forgetting—it always occurs within the context of patterned mind.

# CONSCIOUS MIND \
## [FORGETTING \remembering]

How many times I've wanted
to forget you, forget

the things you told me in the dark
sweet scents of your body, the bouquet

of enchantment in each flower
we knew together

elusive and shortlived, overpowered
by the empty habits

that keep life
from flowering. Yet

each time I've tried
to forget you

groggy with sleep or too much drink,
there is the memory of wildflowers

and the faintest rueful scent of you
blossoms in the stalest air.

*—Brian Fawcett*

Henri Bergson argues that memory is not nearly as extraordinary a phenomenon as forgetting: "We no longer have to explain the preservation of the past, but rather its apparent abolition. We shall no longer have to account for remembering but for forgetting."[34] Something of this accounting is at least begun by Jon Elster, who, drawing from Kant, distinguishes between *active negation* and *passive negation*.[35] The following illustrations of Kant help distinguish the two modalities:

> The passive negation of attention is indifference, the active negation is abstraction; in other words, the absence of consciousness of $x$ is something other than the consciousness of the absence of $x$. . . . The passive negation of desire is again indifference, the active negation disgust; we could say that the absence of desire in $x$ is something other than the desire for the absence of $x$.[36]

Elster goes on to explain the relevance of this for the act of forgetting.

> The will to forget is an example of what has been called "to want what couldn't be wanted," an impossibility, since it relies on the confusion of active and passive negation. Forgetfulness, or indifference, is a passive negation—simply the absence of consciousness of $x$—while the will to forget requires the consciousness of the absence of $x$. Wanting to forget is like deciding to create obscurity from light.[37]

If memory is the patterning of information and information is composed of differences that make a difference,[38] then forgetting must have to do with differences that somehow *stop* making a difference. Thus the choice of the word *indifference* for passive negation is most appropriate. With *no-difference* there is no distinction drawn and thus no information: Knotted memories unravel and truly become *not* when they lose relevance.

The trouble is that differences make a difference *because we make them.* Thus, any attempt to *make* a difference *not make a difference* cannot help but make sure that it does. The purposeful effort to make something not matter is an act of what Elster calls *active indifference:*

> Active indifference is . . . active negation hiding behind passive appearance. One could undoubtedly imagine an endless stream of such appearances, each more complex than the preceding one and capable of deceiving a great number of people; never-

theless, they would never be able to ignore their origin in active negation. By affecting indifference—from the first to the $n$th degree—one will never *become* indifferent.[39]

How then does one move from remembering to forgetting? As Elster points out, one cannot simply *feign* indifference and hope that it will catch hold in due course, as this simply underscores the memory.

A husband and wife who decide to stay married after one of them has had a serious affair are faced with precisely this dilemma. They are reminded again and again of the betrayal by the very particularities of their life together—comments, letters, dates, smells, notes, friends, thoughts, books, facial expressions, places, sounds, times of day, tones of voice, films, foods, gifts, arguments, pieces of music, clothes, and so on—and everything they do to put it behind them brings it to the fore. Unable to return to a context of

TRUST / (ASSURANCE/forgetfulness)

the partners continually find themselves braced in the chill of

DISTRUST \ [ACTIVE INDIFFERENCE\reassurances]

Within a context of distrust, efforts to relegate an infidelity to the past will continually configure it in the present. The forced negations of active indifference can never add up to the relaxed negations of forgetfulness, and reassurances that "it will never happen again" fail to dispel uncertainty, fail to assure.

We are condemned to remember what we contrive to forget; the attempt to detach secures the attachment:

TRYING TO FORGET \
    [CONTRIVED DETACHMENT FROM MEMORY\
      condemned attachment to memory]

What are the implications of this for a couple caught in such a bind? If forgetting isn't possible, what is?

Some primary conceptual tools for understanding the relational organization of such entanglements can be found in G. Spencer-Brown's *Laws of Form*. The arithmetic forms he generates spill forth from two general axioms having to do with the nature of distinctions. Axiom 1, "the law of calling," says:

> *The value of a call made again is the value of a call.*
>
> That is to say, if a name is called and then is called again, the value indicated by the two calls taken together is the value indicated by one of them.
>
> That is to say, for any name, to recall is to call.[40]

Calling a name inscribes a boundary which distinguishes it from what it is not. This *difference* between inside (the named) and outside (not the name) creates and constitutes the information (what Spencer-Brown calls the *value*) indicated by the name. Floyd Merrell, commenting on this axiom, points out that by "evoking a name or a word, you automatically cross the boundary *differentiating* that which is inside from that which is outside."[41] A named presence on one side of a distinction is always *made present* by virtue its absence on the other side. D. T. Suzuki traces the recursiveness of the mutuality.

> "A" cannot be itself unless it stands against what is not "A"; "not-A" is needed to make "A" "A," which means that "not-A" is in "A." When "A" wants to be itself, it is already outside itself, that is, "not-A." If "A" did not contain in itself what is not itself, "not-A" could not come out of "A" so as to make "A" what it is. "A" is "A" because of this contradiction.[42]

The first axiom states that to recall is to call: If a name is called again, the same boundary is marked. The same difference recalled indicates the same information value as it did with the first calling—nothing new is added. Because information is a function of the *difference* between the two sides of a distinction, a function of the *separation* between the name and not-the-name (e.g., between "A" and "not-A"), anything that maintains the boundary will retain the information value of the call.

This explains, then, why the desire to forget always evokes the unwanted memory. A person who mistakenly believes a thought ("A") to be somehow self-contained will try to banish it from his or her mind. But such action only reinscribes the boundary between the thought ("A") and its absence ("not-A"); and it is *there,* in the separated connection between the two, that the memory lives:

> each time I've tried
> to forget you
>
> groggy with sleep or too much drink,
> there is the memory of wildflowers
>
> and the faintest rueful scent of you
> blossoms in the stalest air.[43]

It thus begins to make sense how the memory of a significant separation between a husband and wife (such as an affair) can be kept painfully alive for years and even decades, despite (indeed, in large part, because of) the couple's best attempts to bury it.

The pattern

> TRYING TO FORGET \
>  [CONTRIVED DETACHMENT FROM MEMORY \
>   condemned attachment to memory]

is an expression of the analytic matrix

> CONTRACTION \ [SEPARATION\connection]

and as such offers a convenient metaphor for characterizing people's defective relationships to their own and/or other people's symptoms. Requests for therapeutic help almost always reflect a desire on the part of clients to have some "piece" of themselves (or of other people) eradicated. Whether the issue concerns a torn relationship, distressing emotion, unacceptable behavior, nagging uncertainty, unrelenting pain, inappropriate attitude, annoying habit, or aggravating thought, the request for intervention invariably contains, however implicitly, the assumption that the problem, once isolated, can be banished and forgotten.

It should be obvious at this point that any move on the part of a therapist to directly answer such queries—that is, to accept the invitation to more deeply entrench the separation between the client and the symptom he or she desires to forget—will only help spin the vicious circles in which the person is caught that much faster and tighter. The next chapter will discuss how therapists can avoid getting whisked up in such swirls; it describes the means by which one can encounter the short-circuits of contraction with the long-circuits of completion. But first it is necessary to return to the work of Spencer-Brown.

Mind (memory) is composed not of things or even of ideas of things, but of distinctions, of relationships between. As has been discussed, anything that sharpens the *separation* between the two sides of a distinction highlights the difference that defines it and more clearly outlines the edges of the memory constituted by it. It follows, then, that in confirming the *connection* between the two sides of a distinction, a correspondence is established that takes the edge off the differentiation composing the memory. An image carved in bas-relief vanishes when the difference in height between it and its surroundings is sanded smooth. It is to the possibility of such disappearance of information that Spencer-Brown's second axiom, "the law of crossing," alludes:

> *The value of a crossing made again is not the value of the crossing.*
> That is to say, if it is intended to cross a boundary and then it is intended to cross it again, the value indicated by the two intentions taken together is the value indicated by none of them.
> That is to say, for any boundary, to recross is not to cross.[44]

When one of the two sides of a distinction is crossed into, its distinctiveness is underscored (as in calling or recalling) and it becomes foreground to the background of the other:[45] for example, A/not-A. But when the boundary is *recrossed*, each side (A *and* not-A) becomes foreground *and* background:

(**A/not-A**) / (A/not-A)

Foreground — **A/not-A** — and background — A/not-A —are now *identical*, which means that there is no longer a distinction marking them as different or separate. With no difference there is no information. To paraphrase the second axiom: "The information value indicated by the identity of the two sides is the information value indicated by neither of them."

Recrossing *connects* the two sides of a distinction such that the difference becomes *not*. When A and not-A are fully joined, there is neither A nor not-A; unified, with nothing to distinguish one from the other, relata and relationship dissolve. However, the noting (calling) of this unity differentiates *it* from what it is not, and thus puts it on one side (as foreground) of a still more encompassing distinction. The ongoing interplay between recrossing and recalling can thus be arrayed as a pattern of completion. Whereas recrossing reiterates the connection between the two sides of a distinction, re-calling renews the separation:

COMPLETION / (RECROSSING/recalling)

Bateson notes that going beyond the vicious circles of ad-diction, "beyond the double bind," has something to do with the "*completion* of tasks."[46] The issue, then, is not how best to forget a memory or a symptom, but how to gather its pres-ence and absence in such a way as to allow it to complete. An affair cannot be forcefully forgotten, cannot be banished from the history of a relationship, but it *can* be connected to in a different way. Instead of continually recalling distrust (or trying not to recall it, which, as has been explained above, comes to the same end), a couple might find ways of recrossing the distinction between trust and distrust in all aspects—in both the foreground and background—of their relationship.

The notion of how to move from the tight circles of con-traction to the relaxed circling of completion is developed, in the final chapter, primarily within the context of therapy. However, the ability to "go beyond the double bind," to com-plete distinctions, is an art that transcends the formal rela-tionship between client and therapist. It has much to do with being fully and completely alive.

# 4

# From CONTRACTION \

## [SEPARATION \connection]

# to

# COMPLETION /

## (CONNECTION /separation)

夫唯病病是以不病

聖人不病以其病病是以不病

Only one defecting from defection is thereby
    not defective
The sage is not defective—
      defects from defection and is thereby
    not defective
                —*Lao Tzu*

To live by expert advice is to abandon one's life.
                —*Wendell Berry*

Every explicit duality is an implicit unity.
                —*Alan Watts*

Well, what I really said was that I don't know
anybody who could really work Taoism.
                —*Gregory Bateson*

Only by restoring the broken connections can
we be healed. Connection *is* health.
                —*Wendell Berry*

In executing Taoist principles, a therapist risks doing just that—executing them. The Greek root of the word *therapy* means "to heal" (make whole), but as a profession invented by and situated within a fractionated society, therapy cannot escape the hairline fissures of purpose that radiate through that world. In this it cannot fail but to be defective, to fall short of completion.

A systemic or relational approach to therapy is distinguished by its commitment to contextual understanding. Taken seriously, this stance prescribes a double focus. Before we can look at the importance of context *within* the domain of therapy, we must first turn and look without, at the context of which it is a part and to which it contributes:

CONTEXTUAL UNDERSTANDING /
(CONTEXT IN THERAPY / therapy in context)

# THERAPY IN CONTEXT \
## [SPECIALIZATION \ health]

The modern self-seeker becomes a tourist of cures, submitting his quest to the guidance of one guru after another. The "cure" thus preserves the disease.

—*Wendell Berry*

Therapy sets up shop in the schisms of our culture, and, as a business, profits by collecting rent on the rents. Wendell Berry bewails the way experts step into the breach, only to further widen the gap:

The modern urban-industrial society is based on a series of radical disconnections between body and soul, husband and wife, marriage and community, community and the earth. At each of these points of disconnection the collaboration of corporation, government, and expert sets up a profit-making enterprise that results in the further dismemberment and impoverishment of the Creation.[1]

To what extent, then, is therapy itself not just another symptom, a business whose very existence *demands* a continual supply of problems, a solution that by virtue of being a "solution," fails to escape the dichotomous premises of the ills it seeks to cure?

SOCIETAL ADDICTION \
    [DICHOTOMY EMBODIED IN "SOLVING PROBLEMS" \
        existential demand for problems to solve]

A therapy business, whether in the form of a private practice, a clinic, or an institute, is an enterprise and, even if run as a nonprofit organization, has a bottom line to meet. It is therefore organized by what Bateson refers to as the monotone values of money: "Money is always transitively valued. More money is supposedly always better than less money. For example, $1,001 is to be preferred to $1,000."[2] The economics of therapy are thus a *corruption* (from the Latin *cor-*, "together," "altogether," and *rumpere*, "to break," "violate": "to altogether violate") of the principles of its practice. This cannot be taken lightly; the logic of money is *contra naturam* as Ezra Pound would say, and it exacts its toll:

> with usura the line grows thick
> with usura is no clear demarcation[3]

Demarcations have indeed become unclear when practitioners who profess a relational orientation and denounce the dangers of labeling fall back on the insular categories described in the *Diagnostic and Statistical Manual of Mental Disorders*, 3rd Ed. Rev. (DSM-III-R) when it comes time for third-party billing. Instead of lobbying government officials with regard to who should or should not be allowed to diagnose with the DSM-III-R (i.e., who should or should not be allowed to collect third-party payments), why are we not convincing the officials and the insurance companies that there are better ways to organize treatment?

Are there better ways? Or is all treatment defective? Therapy is a profession, and therapists, as professionals, are specialists. Berry considers such expertise the bane of health.

> The disease of the modern character is specialization. Looked at from the standpoint of the social *system,* the aim of specialization may seem desirable enough. . . . The difficulties do not appear until we look at specialization from the opposite standpoint—that of individual persons.[4]

In giving our lives over to the dictates of specialists, we forgo our responsibility for our own health and the health of our world. And in losing our responsibility we lose our freedom. By separating problems into different domains—individual, familial, economic, environmental, political, societal, spiritual, biological, historical, and so on—specialists engender the schisms they study and strive to heal. This gives new, painful meaning to the Heisenberg hook. Berry elaborates:

> The problems thus become the stock in trade of specialists. The so-called professions survive by endlessly "processing" and talking about problems that they have neither the will nor the competence to solve. The doctor who is interested in disease but not in health is clearly in the same category with the conservationist who invests in the destruction of what he otherwise intends to preserve. They both have the comfort of "job security," but at the cost of ultimate futility.[5]

As *specialists of wholeness,* systemically oriented therapists are a living oxymoron: when our knowing of health is particular, we particulate the health of the known. Ignorance of such contracted double binds is a defection (不 知 知 病 *ignorant knowing: defective*) that, like an infection, can spread through the connected patterns of Mind:

ADDICTION TO SPECIALISTS \
    [IGNORANCE OF THE PARTICULATION OF HEALTH \
        particular knowledge of health]

For farmer, farm, and food in the following passage of Berry's, substitute therapist, therapy, and mind:

> If a farmer fails to understand what health is, his farm becomes unhealthy; it produces unhealthy food, which damages the health of the community. . . . The farmer is a part of the community, and so it is as impossible to say exactly where the trouble began as to say where it will end. The influences go backward and forward, up and down, round and round, compounding and branching as they go. All that is certain is that an error introduced anywhere in the network ramifies beyond the scope of prediction.[6]

Such recognition can occasion despair and give rise to efforts to contain or escape the ramiform influence of the errors.[7] But attempts to defect are themselves defective— there is no escape, there are no insular boundaries in a world of recursive connections. Whereas one cannot defect from defects, it *is* possible to defect from defection, to run away from running away—that is, to *stop running,* turn around, and find imaginative ways to *bring defect to effect* (i.e., *effect* in the sense of "accomplishment" or "fulfillment").[8] This is the beginning of making whole, of recrossing distinctions, and it can serve as a guide not only for therapy in context, but context in therapy.

# CONTEXT IN THERAPY /
## (COMPLETION/contraction)

Healing . . . complicates the system by opening and restoring connections among the various parts—in this way restoring the ultimate simplicity of their union. . . . The parts are healthy insofar as they are joined harmoniously to the whole.

—*Wendell Berry*

What is a therapist that a client may consult her, and a client that he may consult a therapist? Clients are clients because they ask therapists for help. But the person asked is the wrong person, and the question posed is the wrong question. Therapy is a process wherein the client learns how to stop being a client by discovering how not to ask the wrong person the wrong question. At the same time, the therapist must learn how to stop being the therapist by not answering the wrong question right away and discovering how to not-answer the wrong question in a right way.

Both the person queried and the question posed are wrong because the act of asking a specialist for help and the nature of the help requested each contribute to the contraction:

THERAPY AS SOLUTION \
    [ATTEMPTING TO ERADICATE (SEPARATE FROM) PROBLEM \
      asking help of (connecting to) specialist]

The therapist responds to such analytic dichotomies by completing distinctions:

THERAPY AS COMPLETING DISTINCTIONS /
    (BRINGING DEFECT TO EFFECT /
      not-answering dichotomous questions)

*Con-versation* (turning together) within this latter matrix creates a context in which the *chasmal* can become *chiasmal.*[9]

Bradford Keeney and Jeffrey Ross describe how to listen cybernetically to client requests in terms of the complementarity *change/stability:*

> A cybernetic view of multiple communication in systemic therapy begins with the assumption that troubled systems present multiple communications, sometimes taken as contradictory, to a therapist. These communications include: "change us" and "stabilize us." These two communications, when viewed as a double description, mark the recursive complementarity of a cybernetic system. In effect, dual requests for stability and change are a way of indicating that the system is exploring the possibility of altering the way it changes in order to remain stable.[10]

They then go on to suggest the implications of this for structuring interventions:

> A cybernetic view of therapeutic intervention suggests that a therapist mirror the multiple communications a troubled family presents. Accordingly, therapists may inform families to change *and* stabilize. . . . These messages are not contradictory, nor do they involve a logic of negation, but are connected through a logic of complementarity.[11]

Therapeutic conversation is interpreted slightly differently if it is considered a contrapuntal interaction of contraction and completion. Because clients' connections are contextualized by separation, their requests for change can be expected to be similarly divisive—change will be thought separable from stability. In asking for help to "change this symptom or that family member, while leaving everything and/or everyone else as is," they are expecting a dichotomous solution to a schismatic dilemma. And indeed, any direct response to such a request will be contextualized by the premises of the question and thus will necessarily remain chasmal in form.[12] A chiasmal response—in which change and stability are recursively *connected* within a context of completion—requires, in the not-acting spirit of *wu wei,* that the question be *not-answered.*

Alan Watts affirms that "there is no direct answer to an irrational question" and "As we say, 'Anyone who goes to a psychiatrist ought to have his head examined!' In other words, his problem is his question, his belief that the question he is asking makes sense."[13] To be healing, the therapist must turn people back to their questions in a way that is not merely a recalling (for to recall is to call again and to stay stuck in contraction) but a recrossing. The resulting completion will be formally related to long-circuited *inversions* of contraction—to what Bateson refers to as "adaptations of high logical type, transcending . . . double-binds."[14]

## LONG-CIRCUITS / (DISCIPLINE / *wu wei*)

Not-answering is a form of not-acting, a not-giving-in to requests for immediate (and thus potentially addictive) comfort. Bateson describes the curious behavior of mountain climbers who struggle to the top of a mountain despite heavy packs, growing blisters, and exhaustion.[15] Whereas the commonsense thing to do would be to stop, eat lunch, and turn back (as when addicts give themselves another fix upon suffering the first pangs of withdrawal), they instead press on until reaching the summit. Why do they do this? They obviously have not done away with conscious purpose—they indeed set out to get to the *top* of the mountain—but have properly embedded it as *discipline* in a relationship which includes the mountain itself as part of a long-circuited Mind. Similarly, as Watts illustrates, desire has its place as one moves in the direction of no-desire:

> STUDENT How do I get rid of desire?
>
> TEACHER Do you really want to get rid of it?
>
> STUDENT Yes and no. I want to get rid of the desire that causes anguish; but I do not want to get rid of the desire to get rid of it.[16]

The *wu wei* of the climbers' discipline includes a knowing ignoring (知 不 知) of the pleas and aches of their bodies for quick relief, thus allowing them to complete their ascent and to repair a rift between self and environment, recrossing a distinction that Berry says is usually conceived of as pure separation:

> Once we see our place, our part of the world, as *surrounding* us, we have already made a profound division between it and ourselves. We have given up the understanding—dropped it out of our language and so out of our thought—that . . . our land passes in and out of our bodies just as our bodies pass in and out of our land.[17]

Bateson equates the climbers' discipline of not-answering the screams of the body with the discipline required of the Zen monk:

> Why does the Zen monk sit through hours of agony in the lotus position, his legs getting more and more paralyzed and his head getting more and more addled? And while he does this, why does he contemplate or wrestle with a koan, a traditional paradox, a sort of conceptual double bind?[18]

Watts explains *za-zen* (sitting meditation) as follows:

> It is simply a quiet awareness, without comment, of whatever happens to be here and now. This awareness is attended by the most vivid sensation of "nondifference" between oneself and

the external world, between the mind and its contents—the various sounds, sights, and other impressions of the surrounding environment. Naturally, this sensation does not arise by trying to acquire it; it just comes by itself when one is sitting and watching without any purpose in mind—even the purpose of getting rid of purpose.[19]

Common to both climbing and sitting meditation is the chiasmal discipline of recrossing severed distinctions, of making whole. Long-circuits replace short-circuits. This is the same relentless discipline that Berry deems essential in the maintenance of a working farm:

It's like having a milk cow. Having a milk cow is a very strict discipline and a very trying circumstance. It means you've got to be home twice a day to milk whether you want to or not, or else the cow will be ruined. Some days you'd rather do anything than go down to that barn and maybe some days you go and you're kind of bored with it. But other days it's a most rewarding thing and you realize that you get the reward and happiness of it because you stuck to it when it *wasn't* rewarding. There's some kind of wisdom in that fidelity.[20]

The wisdom is that of completion. The tightly coiled double binds of contraction are unknotted and relaxed (completed) by inverting the contextual layering of separation and connection. This movement—from

CONTRACTION \ [SEPARATION \ connection]

to

COMPLETION / (CONNECTION/separation)

—defines the nature of reversal in therapeutic process.

The chiasmal discipline of the therapist finds expression in the two complementary ways of not-acting mentioned earlier.

1. In *not answering a wrong question right away,* the therapist takes care not to act with haste or unmediated purpose. As in the practice of the Taoist martial art T'ai Chi Ch'üan, most can be learned by staying relaxed, most can be accomplished by acting at the right time, and balance is maintained by not *having* to learn or accomplish anything. As Watts suggests,

> it is a great disadvantage to any therapist to have an ax to grind, because this gives him a personal interest in winning. . . . But we saw, in reference to the Zen master, that he can play the game effectively just because winning or losing makes no difference to him.[21]

Bateson similarly discusses how purposeful manipulation precludes completion:

> If the therapist is trying to take a patient, give him exercises, play various propagandas on him, try to make him come over to our world for the wrong reasons, to manipulate him—then there arises a problem, a temptation to confuse the idea of manipulation with the idea of a cure. . . .
>
> This is, I think, really what these disciplines of meditation are about. They're about the problem of how to get there without getting there by the manipulative path, because the manipulative path can never get there. So, in a way one can never know quite what one is doing.[22]

2. In *not-answering a wrong question in a right way,* the therapist responds at a more encompassing level than the query and thus avoids being organized by its dichotomous premises. Such participation is a *connected separation,* an absorbed detachment that is not engineered by an oppositional pushing away but is inhered in the contextual gap between whole and part. The focus of attention and involvement is not on the level of the particular but on the *relations between,* on the context.

By embracing both sides of all distinctions, chasms are met with chiasms, the recalled is recrossed, and defects are brought to effect. Each of these three contextual responses are simply variations on the same pattern of therapeutic practice, on the discipline of completing distinctions.

## COMPLETING DISTINCTIONS / (CHIASM/chasm) (RECROSSING/recalling) (EFFECT/defect)

Now, I can't tell you the right answers—in fact, I'm not sure I would if I could, because, you see, to tell you the real answers, to know the real answers, is always to switch them over to that left brain, to the manipulative side. And once they're switched over, no matter how right they were poetically and aesthetically, they go dead, and become manipulative techniques.

—*Gregory Bateson*

To go in the dark with a light is to know the light.
To know the dark, go dark. Go without sight,
and find that the dark, too, blooms and sings,
and is traveled by dark feet and dark wings.

—*Wendell Berry*

As has been pointed out a number of times, there are important limits to what can and should be said about patterns of completion. When a constellated relationship—be it wildflower, sonata, idea, poem, or conversation—is encountered in context as a composed whole, it comes alive. Analytically explicated, the connections are severed and it dies.

It is with this understanding that the following case is presented. Not intended as an exhaustive illustration of the ideas developed in the book, it can be more appropriately thought of as a kind of melodic variation on some of the themes. The commentary will serve as program notes, providing background material and suggestions for how to listen.[23]

A woman in her mid-forties asked me (who, as a therapist, was the wrong person) the following wrong (divisive) question: "How can I get the panic-depressions [her term] that have been plaguing me under control?" Not-answering her right away took one meeting, not-answering her in a right way took three months. That is, the necessary context for completion was able to be established in the initial session; however, the process itself, always unpredictable, took place in its own time.[24]

At the time of her first appointment, Lynn had been divorced from Edward, her husband of twenty-four years, for two years, and she was living with her twenty-year-old daughter. Her son, Brian, sixteen, had headed up the coast a month earlier to live with his father in a different state. Although inconvenienced by, and embarrassed about, crying unexpectedly at work, Lynn was most concerned about the three recent panic-depressions that had occurred without warning when she was alone at home. Each one lasted about two hours and left her feeling frightened and drained. She had had somewhat similar "anxiety attacks" when she was married, but they had stopped after her divorce.

THERAPIST  When they happen, what do you think about? What goes through your mind?

CLIENT  Oh God, what do I think about? [pause] I think about killing myself.

THERAPIST  Mm-hmm.

CLIENT  And I talk myself out of it.

THERAPIST  And when you're thinking about killing yourself,

you said earlier—like thoughts of not having friends—what . . .

CLIENT But I do have friends.

THERAPIST Okay, but just, what sorts of . . . Do you think about Brian? Or do you think about your husband, or any person in particular?

CLIENT No, I don't. I think that it's, um, it's just too big a bitch to live. It isn't really hinged on anybody else.

THERAPIST So you go . . .

CLIENT I just, uh, that's all it is. And then I feel, I'm real good at guilt so I think "oh God" you know. The guilt of how I might, what I might do to my children is my saving, my, you know, is what I hinge it on.

THERAPIST With Brian gone, does that make that safety net less safe?

CLIENT No, no. Because I don't think of them, how if I kill myself, they won't see me or anything on that basis. I think of the psychological impact on their lives.

Suicide, the ultimate separation, is a logical chasmal solution within a world of CONTRACTION \ [SEPARATION \ connection], and guilt can at best be an attenuated connection within such a context:

PANIC-DEPRESSION \ [SUICIDE \ guilt]

It could have been that talking about—or even the implicit suggestion of—the potential of committing suicide was serving as its own connection to her daughter, ex-husband, or son:

PANIC-DEPRESSION \

[SUICIDE \ messages about potential suicide]

But this avenue of exploration turned out to be a blind alley: Her contact with her son and husband was minimal and perfunctory, and her relationship with her daughter was cordial but uninvolved—they were, as she put it, like roommates.

Asked about her creative interests, Lynn spoke of her work as an interior designer, a profession she had begun before marrying Edward; during their time together she had planned and helped build two of their homes. She also liked to write, but had stopped of late. The following was offered as an explanation:

> CLIENT It's just when I'm thinking and speaking, I think there's perhaps covering up and denial going on.[25] It's not as authentic. When I write I read it back and I go "oh that's too, that is too close! I didn't mean to get that close to that. I'm not doing this anymore!"
>
> THERAPIST When did you stop?
>
> CLIENT Uh, well I, actually I think something, what you're talking about may be, with these panic attacks, they might have been somewhat triggered by my writing. I'm not, there may be a correlation, I can't quite remember, but I'm thinking that that might have something to do with it.
>
> THERAPIST And you said they happen with the [unclear], is that what you said?
>
> CLIENT Yah.
>
> THERAPIST And so you've just in the last couple of days stopped writing, or . . . ?
>
> CLIENT Yah, I mean I'm just, I'm working and sleeping and working and sleeping, I just try not to do anything but that. I'm avoiding myself [laugh]. I mean I know that I'm doing that, I mean I'm not. It's not anything, you know. It's no great shock to me that I'm doing that. But that, but I can't afford to write right now.
>
> THERAPIST Can't afford . . .
>
> CLIENT To write.

THERAPIST  Because it's too close?

CLIENT  Yah, yah.

THERAPIST  When you write, is there a particular thing that you write about?

CLIENT  No. Sometimes I just start to write a letter to a friend and the next thing I know I'm writing all this crap down, you know, and I don't really [unclear]. Or I'll write lists, or I try to say "okay, this is what I need to do tomorrow, and this, what I need to do, now what do I, okay, do . . ."

Lynn used separation as an attempt to keep in check something that was beyond her control, something that scared her deeply: "Oh that's too, that is too close! I didn't mean to get that close to that. I'm not doing this anymore!" Not writing and "avoiding" herself were contractions, divisive solutions that had the potential for schismogenic runaway: If even the writing of a list was enough to set the panic off, how long before the picking up of a pencil would become a dangerous act?

The term *panic-depression* is itself indicative of a short-circuit. The simultaneity of panic and depression suggests a tight spinning between the two, each feeding off the other. One way to stop their mutual escalation and to mark the beginning of a long-circuit is to separate them, both conceptually and in time:

THERAPIST  I've got a couple of hunches that I want to check out with you. Because I think that it's significant that you think of what's been happening as panic-depressions. And you're not quite sure how you came up with that name but [unclear]. And, and I think your intuitive sense has been very good, from what you've told me. And in fact that's a very appropriate term, but I think maybe you weren't quite sure why the two were connected.

CLIENT  Yah.

THERAPIST  And I had a couple of hunches. One, I think that the panic, that there is a panic component, and what you've panicked about is the depression.

CLIENT  Makes sense.

THERAPIST  You, you start, when you talk about, with the writing, you start off with something that's organized. It's either organized around writing a letter or writing a list.

CLIENT  Mm-hmm.

THERAPIST  It's very, it's left brain, it's very analytical, and you're an analytical person.

CLIENT  Mm-hmm.

THERAPIST  And what happens is ideas and feelings and thoughts start flowing out of that and it breaks away from the structure, . . .

CLIENT  Mm-hmm.

THERAPIST  . . . and it's free flowing and then you look at that and you say "oh shit!"

CLIENT  Yah, exactly.

The differentiation of panic and depression allows the vicious circle of Lynn's contraction to be more clearly layered as:

DEPRESSION \ [PANIC \ flow of thoughts and feelings]

Her panic was a function of a chasmal separation, a pushing away that *actively negated* her connected flow of depressing thoughts and feelings. This same pattern of solution was then applied to the panic itself, as she attempted to control *it* through distance (not-writing, avoidance). Doomed to failure, this could only lead to panic about the panic.

There is but a slight difference between contraction and completion, a small shift whereby the tight composition of the former becomes the relaxed composure of the latter: Chasm becomes chiasm when the imbrication of separation and connection is inverted:

CONTRACTION \ [SEPARATION \ connection]

becomes

COMPLETION / (CONNECTION/separation)

Of course it makes just as much sense to note that separation and connection invert when a contraction is completed. There is no beginning to a circle; a difference can be introduced anywhere.

The shift in this case came when the short-circuit of depression was recontextualized as a long-circuit of mourning. Having experienced a number of significant losses—most notably the demise of her marriage and, more recently, the departure of her son—it made sense to Lynn that the sadness she was feeling was part of a mourning cycle. Drawing on the traditions and rituals of her religion, it was possible to weave a context in which periods of deep sadness were seen as *natural* and *necessary,* as part of an encompassing healing. This then allowed for a defection from defection; rather than running away from painful thoughts and feelings, she could turn around and embrace them.[26] Separation within mourning is a *passive negation,* a letting go that happens when it doesn't have to, when memories are gathered up rather than pushed away:

DEPRESSION (VICIOUS CIRCLE) \
[PANIC \ connected flow *of* thoughts and feelings]

becomes

MOURNING (COMPLETE CIRCUIT) /
(CONNECTION *TO* THOUGHTS AND FEELINGS / letting go)

THERAPIST  It's a little bit like sleeping. If you say "I don't want to sleep, I'm just going to be organized and I'm going to work twenty-four hours a day," at

CLIENT      some point in time you're going to fall asleep.

CLIENT      Yes, that makes sense, yes.

THERAPIST      Okay, so if you say "I'm not going to have these panic-depressions and I'm just going to control myself and make sure I don't have them" and you get tight and tight, they're going to happen. Because they're important and necessary. So, obviously, the thing to do is: You plan your sleep time; you also plan sad time. Plan mourning time. 'Cause see if you have them, if you have them for half an hour a day . . .

CLIENT      You're saying have them on my terms, and not on their terms, is what you're saying.

THERAPIST      Yah, mm-hmm.

This is an example of answering a wrong question in a wrong way. Having panic-depressions on *her* terms maintains the notion of control and thus oppositional distance. It would have been more appropriate to have said: "Plan them to *ensure* they happen. Protect time for them."

Defect was brought to effect through Lynn's writing, the activity she had identified as triggering her panic-depressions. The spiral runaway she described began with something structured—a list or a letter. At some point memories and ideas would begin to pour forth, she would get "too close" and, frightened, push them away. The pattern of this sequence—structure, flow, panic—was slightly modified and given back to her as an activity of mourning. Lynn was asked to begin her grieving time by writing something structured, to wait for it to break off into a flow of thoughts and feelings, and when she had enough material with which to work, to structure the flow into a poem. By folding the process back on itself—structure, flow, structure—the writing provided its own calibration, and control via separation was no longer necessary.

| | |
|---|---|
| CLIENT | I'm not going to have any problem with the flow. Read, reading what I've written is going to be what knocks me for a loop. I mean I know that, I mean because that's what always happens. |
| THERAPIST | Okay. |
| CLIENT | And then having to deal with that and condense it, um . . . |
| THERAPIST | So what you might want to do, what you might want to do is only allow yourself to write for five minutes. |
| CLIENT | Okay. |
| THERAPIST | And then that will give you twenty-five minutes to form it into a poem, it won't give you as much to work with. |
| CLIENT | Because there's always redundancy in it anyway. |
| THERAPIST | So, however, but there has to be both. |
| CLIENT | Okay. |
| THERAPIST | There has to be both. Then, and *this* is mourning. See what I want you to do, what I, I want the flow to be centered on loss. |
| CLIENT | Okay. |
| THERAPIST | I don't want you to say "what a bastard the guy I had at work today was." Okay? And it can be the loss of your marriage, or of Brian, or of your cat when you were seven. |

By the end of this first session a context had been established in which the dichotomous distinction between Lynn's *self* and her *heart's reasons*[27] could be recrossed, and her short-circuited responses could be relaxed and extended in time. Subsequent meetings and suggestions served to reiterate these chiasms.

The panic-depressions ceased after the first meeting, and Lynn began to notice some changes. For one, the black-and-white nightmares she had been having had diminished significantly, and in their stead came colorful dreams which were, for her, "positive signs of hope." Nevertheless, a number of weeks later she plummeted into some dark times which scared her, and she began the fifth session describing a recent nightmare, one she had had many times before.

CLIENT   All my life I've had one reoccurring dream, which is, apparently is not a dream, but something that happened when I was very, very, very young and in an air-raid shelter. But you know what "Bird's Eye Custard" is if you're from Canada, probably.

THERAPIST   [shakes head; no]

CLIENT   It's sort of a, it's a warm vanilla pudding, it's like a sauce.

THERAPIST   Oh yah.

CLIENT   Okay. And I remember, I don't remember this but I've always had this reoccurring nightmare where they're dishing it out and and and it's and it's in this sort of damp wet place and I'm in a high-chair. And they ladle it out, and you know how when you were children you get to the bottom and you ladle it and you give, you know, two ladles, two ladles, and then half a ladle, half a ladle, half a ladle, and then quarter of a ladle, quarter of a ladle, it, you know what I'm talking about. Well get it all ladled out and there's this enormous explosion, and there's all this noise and the ceiling shakes and dirt falls down into *my* [unclear] pudding. . . . But, it after a long time, I must have been eleven or twelve, before my grandfather died, I woke up one time and he finally said, "You have these reoccurring 'bout time, nightmares, you 'bout time you told me about them." And I said, "It's always the same one." He said, "It happened to you when you were about seven months old." Okay? I still have those.

Connected to her mourning, Lynn's recent experiences of despair could be contextualized as necessary excursions into the darkness of her loss. Her task when they happened next would be to once again defect from defection and run *toward* that which she had previously run *from*.

THERAPIST   So in terms of giving you "coming attractions" . . .

CLIENT   [laughs]

THERAPIST   . . . uh, it would be that . . .

CLIENT   [sighs deeply, and then whispers] Do you know how *scared* that I get?

THERAPIST   And and it's, and I understand feeling scared, because you're experiencing things that you don't understand. But the piece that you must add to that is an appreciation that not understanding and being afraid is an important and healthy part of what's going on.

CLIENT   [emphatically] That's all right, I just don't want to wake up dead in the morning!

THERAPIST   You won't.

CLIENT   By mistake!

THERAPIST   You won't.

CLIENT   Okay [nods].

THERAPIST   If, if, if you, if you deal with what's happening now by trying to climb out of it . . .

CLIENT   [sighs]

THERAPIST   . . . then it will feel like quicksand. But if you turn around—and you've been doing this—and you walk toward it and you dive into it, and you jump into it, and you work to make the uncontrolled happen, then you're going to start the momentum of that circular turning.

CLIENT   [nods, pause, nods]

THERAPIST   Now I don't know, I don't know where you are in terms of how much deeper you're going to go. It could be the next time you go down, it, it could be further than you went the last time.

CLIENT   I know it will be.

THERAPIST   And, and so when you go into there—there's a quote that I'd like to remember for you . . .

CLIENT   [quietly] I just want to be able to trust myself that [unclear] I am going to surface. I'm willing to do it.

THERAPIST   If you go in with a flashlight, you'll be robbing yourself of the, of the full benefits that you can bring out. It's like going into a deep cave, if you go in with a flashlight you can see some of the things better, but that's the analytical part, the the ordering part wanting to make sense of . . .

CLIENT   I'm trying not to do that.

THERAPIST   So when you go down, you might bring your flashlight for a little ways, but at some point what I'd like you to do is take the flashlight and say "what the hell" and throw the flashlight away.

CLIENT   [nods]

THERAPIST   And take down with you, as a guide, not light— 'cause the light will come up once you start back up—so you don't need to take the . . .

CLIENT   So it *is* like drowning . . . kind of.

THERAPIST   Except that when you're drowning what, what you do to stop drowning is you, you have to make this incredible effort to come up. And what you're doing is here is making an incredible effort to go down.

CLIENT   Okay.

THERAPIST   So if you get, if you get scared, the place to go running is further down.

CLIENT    What do I do when I can't breathe?

THERAPIST    Go further down.

CLIENT    Okay.

THERAPIST    Because, you see it's not like this [moves hand straight down], it's never like that. It's like this [hand inscribes the bottom half of a circle, going down and then back up]. And the further you go down, the further you go up.

With this understanding, the contraction of her continually recalled nightmare could be recrossed, its defect brought to effect by two small, but significant, shifts in the pattern.

THERAPIST    But I'd also like you to have a dream. [pause] I'd like you to have a dream of being in the shelter—in the bomb shelter. As a young child. And when the pudding has been spooned out, I want you to quick!, quick, quick as a bunny, *take a little dirt and pour it on your pudding.* [turns cupped hand over, miming a pouring motion, holds the overturned hand in mid-air, and waits]

CLIENT    [eyes go wide, face muscles slacken, and says in a small voice] Okay. [pause, breathes out heavily, nods, and then says softly] I'll try.

THERAPIST    [long pause] My guess is *that* dream will be in color.

CLIENT    [breathes out sharply two times and inclines her head to the side]

In the following week, Lynn followed through on a plan she had long nurtured. She flew to a city she particularly loved, found a job and a house to rent, and made inquiries about enrolling in the university there. She returned for two subsequent appointments, each of which elaborated the long-circuit already described. A month later she moved, presumably having learned how to not-ask the right question of the right person—herself.

# COMPLETION /
## (CONNECTION/separation)

The differences must be expressed directly, with no vagueness or ambiguity. The unity, on the other hand, must never be expressed: it must be overheard, seen in a glass darkly, felt like a breath of wandering air. So it is well said,

> The unity is to be seen: afterwards, all the
> differences. This is the function of the poet.
> —*R. H. Blyth*

What, then, is a complete action? It is, I think, an action which one takes on one's own behalf, which is particular and complex, real not symbolic, which one can both accomplish on one's own and take full responsibility for. There are perhaps many such actions.

> —*Wendell Berry*

For the writing of this book to be a complete action it was essential that it not be organized as a response to Gregory Bateson's criticisms of family therapy. Regardless of whether the critique was supported or the field defended (or whether there was a shuffling back and forth between in an attempt to be "objective"), this work could not have moved outside the context established by the initial questions raised.

And yet Bateson's concerns *were* voiced and the questions *were* asked—so how could the writing *not* have been contextualized by them? *This* was the question, the challenge, posed by chapter 1—the question that has taken so many pages to not-answer. And it is the very same issue faced and embraced by Taoists, Zen Buddhists, and therapists. To wit: The knowing act of marking a distinction is a distinct act of marked knowing. Given that to mark is to be marked, how can we mark without being marked? How can we remember to forget? Find loss? Desire to not-desire? Hate hate? Act to not-act? Grasp how to let go? Not get caught trying not to get caught?

As a defection from defection, not-answering is a strategy of con-volution, a recrossing of the distinction created by the question, a response that is neither and both an answer and not-an-answer. The discipline of such completion is a discipline of un-discipline. Ma-tsu, a teacher who lived in the early part of the Tang dynasty (618–906 C.E.), chides:

> The Tao has nothing to do with discipline. If you say that it is attained by discipline, finishing the discipline turns out to be losing the Tao. . . . If you say there is no discipline, this is to be the same as ordinary [unliberated] people.[28]

This discipline of freedom is, in Gary Snyder's terms, the "real work" of living:

> What is the real work? . . . It's good to work—I love work, work and play are one. . . . The real work is what we really do. And what our lives are. . . .
>
> [The real work is] to take the struggle on without the *least* hope of doing any good. To check the destruction of the interesting and necessary diversity of life on the planet so the dance can go on a little better for a little longer.[29]

The real work, the disciplined play of not-acting, connects separations and separates connections with the indifferent committment of an imaginative rigor and the committed indifference of a rigorous imagination. Mind—living—resides in *the relation between*.

# NOTES

## Chapter 1.  The Relation Between

1. Gregory Bateson, *Steps to an Ecology of Mind*, p. 1.
2. See, for example, a number of essays reprinted in Bateson, ibid. (including "Style, Grace, and Information in Primitive Art," pp. 128–52; "Social Planning and the Concept of Deutero-Learning," pp. 159–76; and "Toward a Theory of Schizophrenia," pp. 201–77); Gregory Bateson, *Mind and Nature;* and Gregory Bateson and Mary Catherine Bateson, *Angels Fear.*
3. Mary Catherine Bateson, *With a Daughter's Eye*, p. 113.
4. See Alan Watts, *In My Own Way*, p. 387. Steve Heims ("Gregory Bateson and the Mathematicians," p. 150) views Bateson's relationship in the early 1950s with Watts as an important influence: "Typically for Bateson, he was drawing his ideas from a mathematician [Norbert Wiener] on the one hand, and from a student of oriental mysticism [Watts], on the other."
5. See M. C. Bateson, *With a Daughter's Eye*, and David Lipset, *Gregory Bateson: The Legacy of a Scientist.*
6. Gregory Bateson, "Intelligence, Experience, and Evolution," p. 50. Bateson's initial statement refers to the correspondence in form between processes of learning and processes of evolution.
7. Bateson, *Mind and Nature*, p. 97.
8. Heinz von Foerster relates that the participants came from the disciplines of psychiatry, engineering, physiology, anthropology, computer science, neurophysiology, zoology, psychology, sociology, philosophy, mathematics, biophysics, electronics,

and anatomy (quoted in Lynn Segal, *The Dream of Reality,* p. 160).

9. Bateson ("The Birth of a Matrix or Double Bind and Epistemology," in Milton M. Berger, ed., *Beyond the Double Bind,* p. 52) uses the term "'cybernetic' to describe complete circuiting systems."

10. Gregory Bateson, "From Versailles to Cybernetics," in *Steps,* p. 476.

11. See Steve J. Heims, "Gregory Bateson and the Mathematicians." As Jay Haley comments ("Plenary Session Dialogue," in Berger, *Beyond the Double Bind,* p. 192): "Looking back, I think Bateson introduced the idea of levels of communication into human and animal behavior. He keeps giving other people credit for it, but I don't know anybody else who introduced it before him. He also introduced the idea that when you do communicate on levels, these levels can conflict."

12. Bateson, *Mind and Nature,* p. 210.

13. Gregory Bateson, "Effects of Conscious Purpose on Human Adaptation," in *Steps,* p. 245.

14. Gregory Bateson, Don D. Jackson, Jay Haley, and John H. Weakland, "Toward a Theory of Schizophrenia," reprinted in *Steps,* pp. 201–27.

15. See Gregory Bateson, "Minimal Requirements for a Theory of Schizophrenia," in *Steps,* pp. 244–70; "Double Bind, 1969," in *Steps,* pp. 271–78; "The Birth of a Matrix," in Berger, *Beyond the Double Bind,* pp. 39–64; "Theory versus Empiricism," in Berger, *Beyond the Double Bind,* pp. 234–37.

16. Gregory Bateson and Jurgen Ruesch, *Communication,* p. 179. Bateson gives credit to Warren McCulloch for first proposing that messages can be seen in terms of report and command (Bradford P. Keeney and Frank N. Thomas, "Cybernetic Foundations of Family Therapy," in Fred P. Piercy and Douglas H. Sprenkle, eds., *Family Therapy Sourcebook,* p. 263).

17. Jay Haley ("Development of a Theory," in *Reflections on Therapy and Other Essays,* p. 43) dates the change to 1958.

18. Gregory Bateson, "A System's Approach," p. 242. Family ther-

apy arose not only in the Bateson project. Psychiatrists such as Ackerman, Bowen and Wynne, Boszormenyi-Nagy, Lidz, and Whitaker were, in the same time period, each initiating family sessions at their various locations around the United States.

19. Lipset, *Gregory Bateson*, p. 215.
20. Ibid., p. 237. Letter from Gregory Bateson to E. G. Mishler, 22 May 1964.
21. Bateson, "Theory versus Empiricism," in Berger, *Beyond the Double Bind*, p. 237.
22. Bateson, "Minimal Requirements for a Theory of Schizophrenia," in *Steps*, p. 269.
23. Bradford P. Keeney, "Gregory Bateson: A Final Metaphor," p. 1.
24. Bateson and Bateson, *Angels Fear*, p. 204.
25. Bateson, "Social Planning and the Concept of Deutero-Learning," in *Steps*, p. 163.
26. See Gregory Bateson, "A Re-examination of 'Bateson's Rule,'" in *Steps*, pp. 379–95.
27. Bateson and Bateson, *Angels Fear*, pp. 204–5.
28. Bateson, "Double Bind, 1969," in *Steps*, p. 273.
29. Stewart Brand, "Both Sides of the Necessary Paradox," p. 28.
30. Gregory Bateson, "Pathologies of Epistemology," in *Steps*, p. 479.
31. In Gyomay M. Kubose, *Zen Koans*, pp. 156, 69, 31, and 30 respectively.
32. See, for example, Alan Watts, *The Way of Zen*, and Arthur F. Wright, *Buddhism in Chinese History*.
33. Yu-lan Fung, *A History of Chinese Philosophy: Volume 1*, p. 175.
34. Opinions vary as to dates. See John Blofeld, trans., *I Ching*; Yu-lan Fung, *A History of Chinese Philosophy*; Iulian K. Shchutskii, *Researches on the I Ching*; Alan Watts, *Tao: The Watercourse Way*; Hellmut Wilhelm, *Change: Eight Lectures on the I Ching*; Richard Wilhelm, trans., *The I Ching or Book of Changes*.
35. John C. H. Wu, trans., *Lao Tzu: Tao Te Ching*; Burton Wat-

son, trans., *The Complete Works of Chuang Tzu;* Titus Yü and Douglas Flemons, trans., *I Ching: A New Translation.*
36. L. Wieger, *Chinese Characters,* p. 789.
37. Ibid., p. 326.
38. Watts, *Tao: The Watercourse Way,* p. 40.
39. Bateson, "A Systems Approach," p. 244.

*Chapter 2.* COMPLETION

1. Gregory Bateson, *Mind and Nature,* p. 147.
2. Francisco J. Varela, *Principles of Biological Autonomy,* p. 84.
3. Bateson, *Mind and Nature,* pp. 7–8.
4. Gregory Bateson, "Form, Substance, and Difference," in *Steps to an Ecology of Mind,* p. 457.
5. Ibid.
6. Varela, *Principles of Biological Autonomy,* p. 84.
7. Morris Berman, *The Reenchantment of the World,* p. 355.
8. Abraham H. Maslow, *The Psychology of Science,* p. 119.
9. Floyd Merrell, *Semiotic Foundations,* p. 11.
10. Benjamin Lee Whorf, "Language, Mind, and Reality," in J. B. Carroll, ed., *Language, Thought, and Reality,* p. 262.
11. Gregory Bateson, "Afterword," in John Brockman, ed., *About Bateson,* p. 244.
12. See especially: Gregory Bateson, *Steps to an Ecology of Mind;* Wendell Berry, *Home Economics;* Morris Berman, *The Reenchantment of the World;* Abraham Maslow, *The Psychology of Science;* Alan Watts, *Psychotherapy East and West;* Anthony Wilden, *System and Structure.*
13. Maslow, *The Psychology of Science,* p. 119.
14. Bateson, "Form, Substance, and Difference," in *Steps,* p. 462.
15. Berry, *Home Economics,* p. 9.
16. Watts, *Psychotherapy East and West,* pp. 19–20.
17. Berman, *The Reenchantment of the World,* p. 108.
18. Ibid., p. 125.
19. Gregory Bateson, "The Cybernetics of 'Self': A Theory of Alcoholism," in *Steps,* p. 313.

20. Ibid., p. 310.
21. Wilden, *System and Structure*, p. 210.
22. Berry, *Home Economics*, pp. 69–70.
23. Gregory Bateson, "The Roots of Ecological Crisis," in *Steps*, p. 493.
24. Kenneth Burke calls the shifting between "a part of" and "apart from" an "unassuming miracle-worker": "It can so readily function as a tiny difference that can make a world of difference. . . . Its susceptibilities admonish us to recall that while we are all 'a part of' our natural environment, there is also a notable respect in which each of us is 'apart from' it, and even apart from the others of our own kind" ("Addendum on Bateson," in Carol Wilder and John H. Weakland, eds., *Rigor and Imagination*, p. 342). The interplay is between separation and connection.
25. Francisco J. Varela, "Not One, Not Two"; and *Principles of Biological Autonomy*. In keeping with Varela's usage, *hegelian* is left uncapitalized.
26. Ibid.
27. Varela, "Not One, Not Two," p. 63.
28. The notion of logical types is discussed in chap. 1.
29. Bateson, "Minimal Requirements for a Theory of Schizophrenia," in *Steps*, p. 267.
30. Varela, *Principles of Biological Autonomy*, p. 102.
31. Varela, "Not One, Not Two," p. 64.
32. Ibid.
33. Quoted in Lynn Segal, *The Dream of Reality*, p. 164.
34. Bateson, *Mind and Nature*, p. 222.
35. This characterization of whole/part distinctions has obviously been significantly influenced by Varela ("Not One, Not Two"; *Principles of Biological Autonomy*) and owes much to the work of Bradford Keeney (*Aesthetics of Change*); however, I make a departure in explicitly contextualizing whole/part complementaries as an expression of the relationship between connection and separation. I have also developed somewhat

different conventions for representing and discussing the layered patterns of complementary relationships (see below).

36. See Douglas R. Hofstadter, *Gödel, Escher, Bach,* pp. 310–36, for a unique and engaging presentation of much the same idea.

37. "Not One, Not Two" is the title of Varela's 1976 article.

38. R. H. Blyth, *Haiku,* p. ix.

39. Quoted in Milton M. Berger, ed., *Beyond the Double Bind,* p. 82.

40. Bateson, *Mind and Nature,* p. 242.

41. Berry, *Home Economics,* p. 10.

42. Ibid., pp. 11–12.

43. Wendell Berry, "The Cold," in *Collected Poems,* p. 59.

44. See Bateson, *Mind and Nature,* pp. 88–90.

45. See Bateson, *Mind and Nature.*

46. Ibid., pp. 157–58.

47. Adapted from John C. H. Wu, trans., *Lao Tzu: Tao Teh Ching,* p. 3; Wing-Tsit Chan, trans., *The Way of Lao Tzu,* p. 101; and Titus Yü, personal communication, spring 1981. I have omitted the semicolons that usually grace the end of each line, as the parallel structure and paratactic juxtaposition of the phrases are adequately indicated by their placement on separate lines. The words *presence* and *absence* render *yu* 有 and *wu* 無 respectively.

48. Adapted from Wu, *Lao Tzu,* chap. 40, p. 59. The word *fan* 反, translated here as "returning," was originally written as 𣎃. According to L. Wieger (*Chinese Characters,* p. 120), it depicts the motion ⌐ of a hand ㇉ turning over. He says it means "to turn over, inversion."

49. Lionel Kearns, postcard to author, 21 April 1985.

50. Bateson, *Mind and Nature,* p. 104.

51. Bateson, "The Cybernetics of 'Self,'" in *Steps,* p. 315.

52. Bateson, *Mind and Nature,* p. 104.

53. Bateson, "Form, Substance, and Difference," in *Steps,* p. 459.

54. Alan Watts, *Tao: The Watercourse Way,* p. 40.

55. Wu, *Lao Tzu*, p. 7. The words "within you" render *chung* 中, or "center."
56. Chung-yuan Chang, *Creativity and Taoism*, p. 19.
57. Lao Tzu says elsewhere (chap. 47) that one can know all under heaven without ever leaving one's door.
58. Watts, *Psychotherapy East and West*, p. 11.
59. Bateson, "Form, Substance, and Difference," in *Steps*, p. 461.
60. Varela, *Principles of Biological Autonomy*, pp. 270–71.
61. Cited in Gregory Bateson and Mary Catherine Bateson, *Angels Fear*, p. 25. The authors actually slightly misquote and mispunctuate the question as: "What is a number that a man may know it: and what is a man that he may know a number?"
62. Bateson, *Mind and Nature*, p. 9.
63. Ibid., p. 12.
64. Bateson, "The Cybernetics of 'Self,'" in *Steps*, p. 313.
65. Ibid.
66. Alasdair MacIntyre, "Ontology," in P. Edwards, ed., *The Encyclopedia of Philosophy: Volume 5*, pp. 542–43.
67. Bateson and Bateson, *Angels Fear*, p. 19.
68. Bateson, *Mind and Nature*, p. 110.
69. Ibid., page 108, footnote.
70. Werner Heisenberg's Uncertainty Principle, formulated in 1927, generalizes the realization that the light needed to observe an electron will itself possess enough energy to knock the electron out of position; the conducting of an experiment alters its own results (Berman, *The Reenchantment of the World*, p. 137).
71. Watts, *Psychotherapy East and West*, p. 88.
72. Berman, *The Reenchantment of the World*, p. 137.
73. Varela, *Principles of Biological Autonomy*, p. 275.
74. Ernst von Glasersfeld, "An Introduction to Radical Constructivism," in Paul Watzlawick, ed., *The Invented Reality*, p. 24.
75. Bateson, *Mind and Nature*, p. 108, footnote.
76. Bateson and Bateson, *Angels Fear*, p. 24.
77. Bateson, *Mind and Nature*, pp. 31–32.

78. Bateson ("Afterword," in Brockman, ed., *About Bateson*, p. 244) himself equates his idea of "difference" with Spencer-Brown's notions of "distinction" and "indication."

79. Bateson, *Mind and Nature*, p. 12.

80. Bateson, "Form, Substance, and Difference," in *Steps*, p. 459.

81. Bateson, *Mind and Nature*, p. 107.

82. Varela, *Principles of Biological Autonomy*, p. 275.

83. Bateson and Bateson, *Angels Fear*, p. 207. G. Bateson (*Mind and Nature*, p. 97, footnote) also uses the term *consciousness* to refer to "that strange experience whereby we (and perhaps other mammals) are sometimes conscious of the products of our perception and thought but unconscious of the greater part of the process."

84. Koans are knotted stories or questions that do not make "conventional" sense. They are given to students in the Zen tradition as part of their practice in breaking out of habits of dichotomous thinking and acting.

85. A play on his phrase, "not one, not two" (see Varela, "Not One, Not Two").

86. Francisco J. Varela, "The Creative Circle," in Watzlawick, *The Invented Reality*, p. 322.

87. See especially Bateson, *Mind and Nature*.

88. G. Spencer-Brown, *Laws of Form*, p. 105.

89. Bateson, "Style, Grace, and Information in Primitive Art," in *Steps*, p. 145.

90. Bateson and Bateson, *Angels Fear*, p. 188.

91. Chan, *The Way of Lao Tzu*, p. 97.

92. Gregory Bateson, "Ecology of Mind: The Sacred," in Rick Fields, ed., *Loka*, p. 24.

93. Chan, *The Way of Lao Tzu*, p. 97.

94. *Tao Te Ching*, chap. 1.

95. *Tao Te Ching*, chap. 14.

96. Bateson, *Mind and Nature*, p. 107.

97. As we shall see later, this question resounds with implications for memory and for therapy.

98. The words *holy, health,* and *whole* share a common etymological root—the Old English word *hal.*

99. Bateson, "Ecology of Mind," in Fields, *Loka,* p. 24.

100. Adapted from Chang (*Creativity and Taosim,* p. 30) and R. H. Blyth (*Zen in English Literature and Oriental Classics,* p. 141).

101. Wu, *Lao Tzu,* chap. 27, p. 37.

102. Bateson, "Afterword," in Brockman, ed., *About Bateson,* p. 244.

103. Bateson and Bateson, *Angels Fear,* p. 28.

104. Gregory Bateson, *Metaphors and Butterflies.* Audio cassette of lecture given at Esalen Institute, 1975.

105. Octavio Paz, *Children of the Mire,* pp. 72–73.

106. Bateson, *Metaphors and Butterflies.*

107. Gregory Bateson, *What Is Epistemology?* Audio cassette of lecture given at Esalen Institute, 1979.

108. Bateson maintains that "poetry is not a sort of distorted or decorated prose, but rather prose is poetry which has been stripped down and pinned to a Procrustean bed of logic" ("Style, Grace, and Information in Primitive Art," in *Steps,* p. 136).

109. From William Carlos Williams, "To Daphne and Virginia," in *Pictures from Brueghel and Other Poems,* pp. 75–76.

110. Bateson, *Mind and Nature,* p. 14.

111. Bateson, "Style, Grace, and Information in Primitive Art," *Steps,* p. 133.

112. It is not surprising that it was a poet who brought a relational understanding to the field of botany, given how exquisitely aware poets must be of the shape of their descriptions.

113. Bateson, *Mind and Nature,* p. 17.

114. Bateson and Bateson, *Angels Fear,* p. 154.

115. Bradford P. Keeney, *On Paradigmatic Change,* p. 16.

116. From William Carlos Williams, "The Desert Music," in *Pictures from Brueghel,* pp. 108–9.

117. *Tao Te Ching,* chap. 64. Wu's *Lao Tzu* (p. 93) served as a

crib, but much verbiage has been eliminated, the form has been streamlined, and the inappropriate male pronouns have been removed. "Doesn't fuss" renders *wu wei* 無 爲 (see below).

118. *Tao Te Ching*, chap. 5.

119. *Tao Te Ching*, chap. 4.

120. Adapted from Wu, *Lao Tzu*, chap. 48, p. 69. The words translated here as "accumulating" 益 and "diminishing" 損 are the respective titles of chapters 42 and 41 of the *I Ching*. In that context they were rendered as "Giving To" and "Taking Away" (Titus Yü and Douglas Flemons, trans., *I Ching*, pp. 153, 150).

121. Bateson and Bateson, *Angels Fear*, p. 81.

122. Blyth, *Haiku*, p. 192. Blyth (p. 28) relates that Ryota (1707–1787) studied Zen under Rito and Ransetsu.

123. John Cage, "Lecture on Nothing," in *Silence*, p. 109.

124. Varela, *Principles of Biological Autonomy*, p. 104.

125. Chan, *The Way of Lao Tzu*, p. 97.

126. This character means both "continuum" and "continuation." The English word *forever* almost contains a "river," an image which Lao Tzu relies on frequently as a metaphor for Tao (e.g., chaps. 8, 28, 32).

127. To appreciate the pun it is necessary to know that *Tao* is pronounced "dow."

128. Berry, *Home Economics*, pp. 4–5.

129. Heinz von Foerster, *Observing Systems*, p. 308.

130. Richard Wilhelm, *Lectures on the I Ching*, p. 7.

131. Titus Yü, personal communication, January 1981.

132. In Ernest Fenollosa, *The Chinese Written Character as a Medium for Poetry*, ed., Ezra Pound, p. 45.

133. Benjamin Hoff, *The Tao of Pooh*, p. 68.

134. Wu's actual rendering of the phrase *wei wu wei* is, in my opinion, a little less compelling: "Do the Non-Ado" (*Lao Tzu*, p. 91).

135. Wu, *Lao Tzu*, p. 53.

136. John Grinder and Richard Bandler, *Trance-formations,* ed., Connirae Andreas, p. 67.
137. Berman, *The Reenchantment of the World,* p. 17.
138. Watson, *The Complete Works of Chuang Tzu,* chap. 19, pp. 204–05.
139. Gary Snyder, *The Real Work,* p. 67.
140. Yü and Flemons, *I Ching,* p. 26.
141. See particularly Bateson, *Mind and Nature.* The story of this puzzle and its interpretative solution is based on the research and analysis conducted by Yü and Flemons in preparing our translation of the *I Ching.*
142. Iulian K. Shchutskii, *Researches on the I Ching,* p. 143.
143. Ibid.
144. Richard Wilhelm, trans., *I Ching or Book of Changes,* p. 369.
145. Shchutskii, *Researches on the I Ching,* p. 136.
146. In contrast, the hypotactic structure of English is hierarchical. In Wilhelm's sentence, *sublime* modifies *success* and is thus subordinate to it.
147. An archaic form of the word *inflame.*
148. Bateson, *Mind and Nature,* pp. 193–94.
149. Ibid., p. 52.
150. Ibid., p. 53.
151. Watson, *The Complete Works of Chuang Tzu,* chap. 22, p. 235.
152. In this sense, *threshold* becomes virtually synonymous with *structure.* See Bateson and Bateson, *Angels Fear.*
153. Bateson, *Mind and Nature,* pp. 114–15.
154. Snyder, *The Real Work,* p. 116.
155. Bateson, *Mind and Nature,* p. 59.
156. Bateson, "Style, Grace, and Information in Primitive Art," in *Steps,* p. 146.
157. *Tao Te Ching,* chap. 22. Adapted from D. C. Lau, trans., *Lao Tzu: Tao Te Ching,* p. 79; and Richard Wilhelm, trans., *Tao Te Ching,* pp. 35–36.
158. Ariane Rump and Wing-Tsit Chan, trans., *Commentary on the Lao Tzu by Wang Pi,* p. 68.

159. Berry, *Home Economics,* p. 15. The artist Harold Towne says precisely the same thing of Picasso: "His genius lay in his timing—he always knew when to stop." (Interview by Peter Gzowski, 22 August 1986. "Morningside" [radio program]. Canadian Broadcasting Corporation.)
160. Wu, *Lao Tzu,* chap. 29, p. 41.

## Chapter 3. CONTRACTION

1. *O. E. D.,* 1971, *s.v.* "defection."
2. Ibid., *s.v.* "defect."
3. The double bind is discussed briefly in chap. 1. See Gregory Bateson, *Steps to an Ecology of Mind,* especially pp. 201–78.
4. Gregory Bateson ("Style, Grace, and Information in Primitive Art," in *Steps,* pp. 128–52) considers feelings to be patterns of relationship, algorithms of the heart or unconscious (see especially p. 140).
5. Roy A. Rappaport, "Sanctity and Adaptation," p. 54.
6. Gregory Bateson, "Effects of Conscious Purpose on Human Adaptation," in *Steps,* p. 445.
7. Gregory Bateson, "Conscious Purpose versus Nature," in *Steps,* pp. 433–34.
8. See Stewart Brand, "Both Sides of the Necessary Paradox."
9. *Tao Te Ching,* chap. 42.
10. Gary Snyder, *The Real Work,* p. 109.
11. Gregory Bateson, "The Cybernetics of 'Self': A Theory of Alcoholism," in *Steps,* p. 335. A Taoist would be more likely to characterize nature in terms of no purpose rather than multi-purposes, but the point is much the same. Cf. also Francisco J. Varela, *Principles of Biological Autonomy,* p. 67, who says that living systems are purposeless.
12. E. E. Cummings, "whatever's merely wilful," in *Complete Poems 1913–1962,* p. 742.
13. Gregory Bateson, "Minimal Requirements for a Theory of Schizophrenia," in *Steps,* p. 265.

14. Gregory Bateson, "A Conversation with Gregory Bateson," in Rick Fields, ed., *Loka*, p. 31.

15. The quote—"Knowing ignorance: tiptop / Ignorant knowing: defective"—is from chap. 71 of the *Tao Te Ching*. The Chinese is read top down and right to left. The words *ignorance* and *ignorant* (from the Latin *in-*, "not" and *gnoscere*, "to know") render the characters *pu chih*—literally "not 不 know 知." The term *tiptop* translates *shang* 上, which means "above" or "up."

16. Bateson, "Style, Grace, and Information in Primitive Art," in *Steps*, p. 146.

17. Paul Watzlawick, John H. Weakland, and Richard Fisch specifically discuss solutions as problems in their book *Change*.

18. Gregory Bateson, "The Birth of a Matrix or Double Bind and Epistemology," in Milton M. Berger, ed., *Beyond the Double Bind*, p. 62.

19. Gregory Bateson and Mary Catherine Bateson, *Angels Fear*, p. 133.

20. Wendell Berry, *Home Economics*, p. 69.

21. Bateson and Bateson, *Angels Fear*, p. 91. The notion of logical types was also discussed briefly in chap. 1.

22. Gregory Bateson, "The Roots of Ecological Crisis," in *Steps*, pp. 488–89.

23. Bateson, "The Cybernetics of 'Self,'" in *Steps*, pp. 310–11.

24. Gregory Bateson, "The Logical Categories of Learning and Communication," in *Steps*, p. 301.

25. See Bateson, *Steps*, and *Mind and Nature*.

26. Berry, *Home Economics*, p. 71.

27. Anthony Wilden, *System and Structure*, p. 222.

28. Berry, *Home Economics*, p. 72.

29. Wilden, *System and Structure*, p. 116.

30. Edward E. Sampson, "The Inversion of Mastery," pp. 35–36.

31. See Bateson, "The Cybernetics of 'Self,'" in *Steps*, especially pp. 320–29.

32. George A. Kelly, *A Theory of Personality*, pp. 62–63.

33. Bateson, "The Cybernetics of 'Self,'" in *Steps,* 318–19.
34. Henri Bergson, *An Introduction to Metaphysics,* p. 153.
35. Jon Elster, "Active and Passive Negation," in Paul Watzlawick, ed., *The Invented Reality,* pp. 175–205.
36. Ibid., p. 182.
37. Ibid., p. 185.
38. Bateson, *Steps; Mind and Nature.*
39. Elster, "Active and Passive Negation," in Watzlawick, *The Invented Reality,* p. 195.
40. G. Spencer-Brown, *Laws of Form,* p. 1.
41. Floyd Merrell, *Semiotic Foundations,* p. 11.
42. D. T. Suzuki, "Existentialism, Pragmatism and Zen," in William Barrett, ed., *Zen Buddhism,* p. 269.
43. Brian Fawcett, "How many times I've wanted," in *Tristram's Book,* p. 52.
44. G. Spencer-Brown, *Laws of Form,* p. 2.
45. In Spencer-Brown's terms, the marking of a distinction creates an *indication,* where one of the two sides becomes primary. Bradford Keeney (in *Aesthetics of Change*) equates indication with the notion of punctuation.
46. Bateson, "The Birth of a Matrix," in Berger, *Beyond the Double Bind,* p. 64.

## Chapter 4. From CONTRACTION to COMPLETION

1. Wendell Berry, *The Unsettling of America,* p. 137.
2. Gregory Bateson, *Mind and Nature,* p. 59.
3. Ezra Pound, "Canto XLV," in *The Cantos of Ezra Pound,* p. 229.
4. Berry, *The Unsettling of America,* p. 19.
5. Ibid., p. 22.
6. Ibid., p. 110.
7. Alan Watts (*Psychotherapy East and West,* p. 98) advises that any system of therapy "which leaves the individual upon one horn of the dualistic dilemma is at best the achievement of courageous despair."

8. Cf. the *O.E.D.* (1971), *s.v.* "effect": "*To bring to effect, carry into effect:* to accomplish, bring to a successful issue." Note that in the epigraph by Lao Tzu at the beginning of this chapter, the words *defecting, defection,* and *defective* all render *ping* 病. As explained earlier, *defect* means "the lack or absence of something essential to completeness" (*O.E.D.*, 1971).

9. The *O.E.D.* (1971) defines *chasmal* as being "of the nature of or belonging to a chasm." It is used here to denote a dichotomous orientation to distinctions. A *chiasm* is an intercrossing or a decussation (*O.E.D.*, 1971). Recalling Spencer-Brown's notion of *recrossing* (*Laws of Form*), the term *chiasmal* can be understood as referring to the recrossing or the completion of distinctions.

10. Bradford P. Keeney and Jeffrey M. Ross, *Mind in Therapy*, p. 53.

11. Ibid.

12. For example, Carl Whitaker (John R. Neill and David P. Kniskern, eds., *From Psyche to System*, p. 205) notes that "the ordinary medical system of replying affirmatively to a request for help by one person in a marriage, excluding the other, may in effect be an intervention favoring divorce."

13. Alan Watts, *Psychotherapy East and West*. The first quote is from page 125, the second from page 129.

14. Gregory Bateson, "The Birth of a Matrix or Double Bind and Epistemology," in Milton M. Berger, ed., *Beyond the Double Bind*, pp. 62–63.

15. Ibid., pp. 62–64.

16. Adapted from Watts, *Psychotherapy East and West*, p. 135.

17. Berry, *The Unsettling of America*, p. 22.

18. Bateson, "The Birth of a Matrix," in Berger, *Beyond the Double Bind*, p. 64. Gary Snyder speculates that the origins of meditation lie in hunting: "Our earlier traditions of life prior to agriculture required literally thousands of years of great attention and awareness, and long hours of stillness" (*The Real Work*, p. 107).

19. Alan Watts, *The Way of Zen*, pp. 152–153.

20. Wendell Berry, "The Plowboy Interview: Wendell Berry," p. 8.
21. Watts, *Psychotherapy East and West*, p. 158.
22. Gregory Bateson, "Ecology of Mind: The Sacred," in Rick Fields, ed., *Loka*, p. 26.
23. The particularities of the case and the general orientation of the approach are necessarily entwined; the commentary will, at times, attempt to point out the differences.
24. The client, Lynn, was seen a total of seven times. The following excerpts are from two of the meetings: the first and the fifth. Names and extraneous details have been changed to protect anonymity. Working relationally with one person is, in many respects, the most demanding of therapeutic situations, but circumstances dictated that she be seen alone.
25. Lynn freely used psychological terminology, and it was thus incorporated into the talk. She had been to a number of therapists in the past.
26. The notion of mourning was an appropriate fit given the specifics of the situation; however, the stacking of Lynn's double bind could have been inverted in other ways as well.
27. Pascal via Bateson (see *Steps*).
28. Cited in Watts, *Psychotherapy East and West*, p. 128.
29. Snyder, *The Real Work*, pp. 81–82.

# BIBLIOGRAPHY

Bateson, Gregory. "Social Planning and the Concept of Deutero-Learning" (1942). Reprinted in *Steps to an Ecology of Mind*, 159–76. New York: Ballantine Books, 1972 (cited hereafter as *Steps*).

———. *Naven: A Survey of the Problems Suggested by a Composite Picture of the Culture of a New Guinea Tribe Drawn from Three Points of View*. 2nd ed. Stanford, Calif.: Stanford University Press, 1958.

———. "Minimal Requirements for a Theory of Schizophrenia" (1959). Reprinted in *Steps*, 244–70.

———. "From Versailles to Cybernetics" (1966). Reprinted in *Steps*, 469–77.

———. "Style, Grace, and Information in Primitive Art" (1967). Reprinted in *Steps*, 128–52.

———. "Conscious Purpose versus Nature" (1968). Reprinted in *Steps*, 426–39.

———. "Effects of Conscious Purpose on Human Adaptation" (1968). Reprinted in *Steps*, 440–47.

———. "Double Bind, 1969" (1969). Reprinted in *Steps*, 271–78.

———. "Pathologies of Epistemology" (1969). Reprinted in *Steps*, 478–87.

———. "Form, Substance, and Difference" (1970). Reprinted in *Steps*, 448–65.

———. "The Roots of Ecological Crisis" (1970). Reprinted in *Steps*, 488–93.

———. "The Cybernetics of 'Self': A Theory of Alcoholism" (1971). Reprinted in *Steps*, 309–37.

———. "The Logical Categories of Learning and Communication" (1971). Reprinted in *Steps*, 279–308.

———. "A Re-examination of 'Bateson's Rule'" (1971). Reprinted in *Steps*, 379–95.

———. "A Systems Approach." *International Journal of Psychiatry* 9 (1971): 242–44.

———. *Steps to an Ecology of Mind*. New York: Ballantine Books, 1972.

———. "A Conversation with Gregory Bateson." In *Loka: A Journal from Naropa Institute*, edited by Rick Fields, 28–34. Garden City, N.Y.: Anchor Books, 1975.

———. "Ecology of Mind: The Sacred." In *Loka: A Journal from Naropa Institute*, edited by Rick Fields, 24–27. Garden City, N.Y.: Anchor Books, 1975.

———. *Metaphors and Butterflies*. Big Sur, Calif.: Esalen Institute, 1975. Speaker. Audio cassette.

———. "Afterword." In *About Bateson: Essays on Gregory Bateson*, edited by John Brockman, 235–47. New York: E. P. Dutton, 1977.

———. "The Birth of a Matrix or Double Bind and Epistemology." In *Beyond the Double Bind: Communication and Family Systems, Theories, and Techniques with Schizophrenics*, edited by Milton M. Berger, 41–64. New York: Brunner/Mazel, 1978.

———. "Intelligence, Experience, and Evolution." *Revision* 1 (Spring 1978): 50–55.

———. "Theory versus Empiricism." In *Beyond the Double Bind: Communication and Family Systems, Theories, and Techniques with Schizophrenics*, edited by Milton M. Berger, 234–37. New York: Brunner/Mazel, 1978.

———. *Mind and Nature: A Necessary Unity*. Toronto: Bantam Books, 1979.

———. *What Is Epistemology?* Big Sur, Cal.: Esalen Institute, 1979. Speaker. Audio cassette.

Bateson, Gregory, and Mary Catherine Bateson. *Angels Fear: Towards an Epistemology of the Sacred*. New York: Macmillan, 1987.

Bateson, Gregory, Don D. Jackson, Jay Haley, and John H. Weakland. "Toward a Theory of Schizophrenia" (1956). Reprinted in *Steps*, 201–27.

Bateson, Gregory, and Jurgen Reusch. *Communication: The Social Matrix of Psychiatry*, 3rd ed. New York: W. W. Norton, 1987.

Bateson, Mary Catherine. *With a Daughter's Eye: A Memoir of Margaret Mead and Gregory Bateson*. New York: Washington Square Press, 1984.

Berger, Milton M., ed. *Beyond the Double Bind: Communication and Family Systems, Theories, and Techniques with Schizophrenics*. New York: Brunner/Mazel, 1978.

Bergson, Henri. *An Introduction to Metaphysics: The Creative Mind*. Translated by Mabelle L. Andison. Totowa, N.J.: Rowman and Allanheld, 1946.

Berman, Morris. *The Reenchantment of the World*. New York: Bantam Books, 1984.

Berry, Wendell. "The Plowboy Interview: Wendell Berry." *Plowboy*, March 1973, 7–12.

———. *The Unsettling of America: Culture and Agriculture*. San Francisco: Sierra Club Books, 1977.

———. *Collected Poems*. San Francisco: North Point Press, 1985.

———. *Home Economics*. San Francisco: North Point Press, 1987.

Blofeld, John, trans. *I Ching*. New York: E. P. Dutton, 1965.

Blyth, R. H. *Haiku*. Tokyo: Hokuseido Press, 1949.

———. *Zen in English Literature and Oriental Classics*. New York: E. P. Dutton, 1960.

Brand, Stewart. "Both Sides of the Necessary Paradox." *Harper's*, November 1973.

Burke, Kenneth. "Addendum on Bateson." In *Rigor and Imagination: Essays from the Legacy of Gregory Bateson*, edited by Carol Wilder and John H. Weakland, 341–46. New York: Praeger, 1981.

Cage, John. *Silence*. Cambridge: MIT Press, 1961.

Chan, Wing-Tsit, trans. *The Way of Lao Tzu*. Indianapolis: Bobbs-Merrill, 1963.

Chang, Chung-Yuan. *Creativity and Taoism*. New York: Harper Colophon, 1963.

Cummings, E. E. *Complete Poems 1913–1962*. New York: Liveright Publishing Corp., forthcoming.

Elster, Jon. "Active and Passive Negation: An Essay in Ibanskian Sociology," translated by Ronald Garwood. In *The Invented Reality: How Do We Know What We Believe We Know? (Contributions to Constructivism)*, edited by Paul Watzlawick, 175–205. New York: W. W. Norton, 1984.

Fawcett, Brian. *Tristram's Book*. Vancouver: *The Capilano Review*, no. 19 (1981).

Fenollosa, Ernest. *The Chinese Written Character as a Medium for Poetry*. Edited by Ezra Pound. San Francisco: City Lights, 1936.

Foucault, Michel. *Language, Counter-Memory, Practice: Selected Essays and Interviews by Michel Foucault*. Edited by Donald F. Bouchard and translated by Donald F. Bouchard and Sherry Simon. Ithaca, N.Y.: Cornell University Press.

Fung, Yu-Lan. *A History of Chinese Philosophy: Volume I (The Period of the Philosophers)*. 2nd ed. Translated by Derk Bodde. Princeton: Princeton University Press, 1952.

Grinder, John, and Richard Bandler. *Trance-formations*. Edited by Connirae Andreas. Moab, Utah: Real People Press, 1981.

Haley, Jay. "Plenary Session Dialogue." In *Beyond the Double Bind: Communication and Family Systems, Theories, and Techniques with Schizophrenics*, edited by Milton M. Berger, 191–96. New York: Brunner/Mazel, 1978.

———. "Development of a Theory: A History of a Research Project." In *Reflections on Therapy and Other Essays*, 1–63. Rockville, Md.: Family Therapy Institute, 1981.

Heims, Steve. "Gregory Bateson and the Mathematicians: From Interdisciplinary Interaction to Societal Functions." *Journal of the History of the Behavioral Sciences* 13 (1977): 141–59.

Hoff, Benjamin. *The Tao of Pooh*. Middlesex: Penguin Books, 1982.

Hofstadter, Douglas R. *Gödel, Escher, Bach: An Eternal Golden Braid*. New York: Basic Books, 1979.

Keeney, Bradford P. *On Paradigmatic Change: Conversations with Gregory Bateson.* Typescript, 1977.

———. "Gregory Bateson: A Final Metaphor." *Family Process* 20 (1981): 1.

———. *Aesthetics of Change.* New York: Guilford Press, 1983.

Keeney, Bradford P., and Jeffrey M. Ross. *Mind in Therapy.* New York: Basic Books, 1985.

Keeney, Bradford P., and Frank N. Thomas. "Cybernetic Foundations of Family Therapy." In *Family Therapy Sourcebook,* edited by Fred P. Piercy and Douglas H. Sprenkle, 262–87. New York: Guilford Press, 1986.

Kelly, George A. *A Theory of Personality.* New York: W. W. Norton, 1963.

Kubose, Gyomay M. *Zen Koans.* Chicago: Henry Regnery, 1973.

Lau, D. C., trans. *Lao Tzu: Tao Te Ching.* Middlesex: Penguin Books, 1963.

Lipset, David. *Gregory Bateson: The Legacy of a Scientist.* Boston: Beacon Press, 1982.

MacIntyre, Alasdair. "Ontology." In *The Encyclopedia of Philosophy, vol. 5,* edited by Paul Edwards, 542–43. New York: Macmillan and The Free Press, 1967.

Maslow, Abraham H. *The Psychology of Science.* New York: Harper and Row, 1966.

Merrell, Floyd. *Semiotic Foundations: Steps Toward an Epistemology of Written Texts.* Bloomington: Indiana University Press, 1982.

Neill, John R., and David P. Kniskern, eds. *From Psyche to System: The Evolving Therapy of Carl Whitaker.* New York: Guilford Press, 1982.

Paz, Octavio. *Children of the Mire: Modern Poetry from Romanticism to the Avant-Garde.* Translated by Rachel Phillips. Cambridge: Harvard University Press, 1974.

———. *The Collected Poems of Octavio Paz: 1957–1987.* Edited and translated by Eliot Weinberger. New York: New Directions, 1987.

Pound, Ezra. "Canto XLV." In *The Cantos of Ezra Pound*, 229–30. New York: New Directions, 1972.

Rappaport, Roy A. "Sanctity and Adaptation." *CoEvolutionary Quarterly*, Summer 1974, 54–68.

Rump, Ariane, and Wing-Tsit Chan. *Commentary on the Lao Tzu by Wang Pi*. Hawaii: University of Hawaii Press, 1979.

Sampson, Edward E. "The Inversion of Mastery." *Cybernetic* 2 (1986): 26–39.

Segal, Lynn. *The Dream of Reality: Heinz von Foerster's Constructivism*. New York: W. W. Norton, 1986.

Shchutskii, Iulian K. *Researches on the I Ching*. Translated by William L. MacDonald, Tsuyoshi Hasegawa, and Hellmut Wilhelm. Princeton: Princeton University Press, 1979.

Snyder, Gary. *The Real Work: Interview & Talks, 1964–1979*. Edited by William Scott McLean. New York: New Directions, 1980.

Spencer-Brown, G. *Laws of Form*. New York: E. P. Dutton, 1979.

Suzuki, D. T. *Zen Buddhism: Selected Writings of D. T. Suzuki*. Edited by William Barrett. Garden City, N.Y.: Doubleday Anchor Books, 1956.

Varela, Francisco J. "Not One, Not Two." *Coevolutionary Quarterly*, Fall 1976, 62–67.

———. *Principles of Biological Autonomy*. New York: Elsevier North Holland, 1979.

———. "The Creative Circle: Sketches on the Natural History of Circularity." In *The Invented Reality: How Do We Know What We Believe We Know? (Contributions to Constructivism)*, edited by Paul Watzlawick, 309–23. New York: W. W. Norton, 1984.

Von Foerster, Heinz. *Observing Systems*. Seaside, Calif.: Intersystems Publications, 1984.

Von Glasersfeld, Ernst. "An Introduction to Radical Constructivism." In *The Invented Reality: How Do We Know What We Believe We Know? (Contributions to Constructivism)*, edited by Paul Watzlawick, 17–40. New York: W. W. Norton, 1984.

Watson, Burton, trans. *The Complete Works of Chuang Tzu.* New York: Columbia University Press, 1968.

Watts, Alan. *The Way of Zen.* New York: Mentor Books, 1957.

———. *Psychotherapy East and West.* New York: Vintage Books, 1961.

———. *In My Own Way.* New York: Vintage Books, 1972.

———. *Tao: The Watercourse Way.* New York: Pantheon Books, 1975.

Watzlawick, Paul, John H. Weakland, and Richard Fisch. *Change: Principles of Problem Formation and Problem Resolution.* New York: W. W. Norton, 1974.

Whorf, Benjamin Lee. *Language, Thought, and Reality: Selected Writings of Benjamin Lee Whorf.* Edited by J. B. Carroll. Cambridge: MIT Press, 1956.

Wieger, L. *Chinese Characters: Their Origin, Etymology, History, Classification and Signification. A Thorough Study from Chinese Documents.* 2d ed. Translated into English by L. Davrout. 1927. Reprint. New York: Paragon and Dover, 1965.

Wilden, Anthony. *System and Structure.* London: Tavistock, 1972.

Wilhelm, Hellmut. *Change: Eight Lectures on the I Ching.* Translated by Cary F. Baynes. Princeton: Princeton University Press, 1960.

Wilhelm, Richard, trans. *The I Ching or Book of Changes.* 3rd ed. Translated from German by Cary F. Baynes. Princeton: Princeton University Press, 1967.

Wilhelm, Richard. *Lectures on the I Ching: Constancy and Change.* Translated by Irene Eber. Princeton: Princeton University Press, 1979.

———, trans. *Tao Te Ching: The Book of Meaning and Life.* Translated from German by H. G. Ostwald. London: Arkana, 1985.

Williams, William Carlos. "To Daphne and Virginia." In *Pictures from Brueghel and Other Poems,* 75–79. Norfolk, Conn.: New Directions, 1962.

———. "The Desert Music." In *Pictures from Brueghel and Other Poems,* 108–20. Norfolk, Conn.: New Directions.

Wright, Arthur F. *Buddhism in Chinese History*. Stanford, Calif.: Stanford University Press, 1959.

Wu, John C. H., trans. *Lao Tzu: Tao Teh Ching*. New York: St. John's University Press, 1961.

Yü, Titus, and Douglas Flemons, trans. *I Ching: A New Translation*. Simon Fraser University, Faculty of Interdisciplinary Studies, Burnaby, B.C. Typescript, 1983.

# CREDITS